DEBT-FREE
— ON —
ANY INCOME

DEBT-FREE
ON
ANY INCOME

Lyle and Tracy Shamo

DESERET
BOOK

SALT LAKE CITY, UTAH

Portions of "To the Boys and to the Men" by Gordon B. Hinckley
© Intellectual Reserve, Inc.
Previously published in the Ensign
Used by permission

Library of Congress Cataloging-in-Publication Data

Shamo, Lyle.
   Debt-free on any income / Lyle Shamo, Tracy Shamo.
     p.   cm.
   Includes index.
   ISBN 1-59038-274-9 (pbk.)
     1. Finance, Personal—United States.   2. Debt—United States.   3. Saving and investment—United States.   I. Shamo, Tracy.   II. Title.
HG179.S428 2004
332.024'02—dc22   2003027094

Printed in the United States of America   72076
Publishers Printing, Salt Lake City, UT

10 9   8   7   6   5   4   3   2   1

Contents

FOREWORD   vii

PREFACE   xi

1. MAKING A CASE AGAINST DEBT   1

2. FREEDOM FROM DEBT—A BEGINNING   7
What Is Debt? • Good Debt • Bad Debt • Interest
• Debt Management Rules • Freedom from Debt

3. HOW TO GET OUT OF DEBT   17
Determining Your Debt-to-Income Ratio • Debt
Elimination: A Three-Step Process

4. THE POWER PAYMENT PLAN   27
The Power Payment Plan: Key to Success

5. OTHER METHODS OF DEBT
ELIMINATION   44
Sell, Trade, or Cash In an Assett • Balance
Transfers • Debt Consolidation Loans •
Home Equity Loans • Summary •
Options to Those with Greater Need

6. **DEBT-FREE: A PHILOSOPHY**   59
Pre-Assessment Quiz

7. **DEBT-FREE PLANNING**   67
Three Keys to Financial Success • What Are
Needs and What Are Wants? • Satisfying Both
Needs and Wants • Survey of Needs and Wants

8. **A MAINTENANCE PLAN**   80
Outsmarting Debt • Building a Maintenance Plan
• Identification of Yearly Peak Expenses •
Identification of Yearly Peak Income • How Much
Are You Worth?

9. **A YEARLY AND MONTHLY PLAN**   93
Your Yearly Financial Plan • Your Monthly Plan •
The Plan and the Tally

10. **FUTURE PLANNING AND CRISIS PLANNING**   144
The Wisdom of Savings • How Do You Save? •
Crisis Planning • Saving in a Debt-Free World

APPENDIX: DEBT-FREE SAVINGS   156
Auto and Transportation • Charity and
Contributions • Debts and Credit Cards •
Education • Food • Gifts • Home and Shelter •
Insurance • Leisure and Recreation • Medical •
Other/Miscellaneous • Personals • Savings and
Investments • Taxes • Utilities • Vacations and
Travel • Wardrobe

INDEX   183

ABOUT THE AUTHORS   189

Foreword

Not long ago, I was asked to review the schedules and spreadsheets contained in this book because of my familiarity with the programs used. My review was largely technical in nature. As I reviewed each chapter and aligned the computer models to match the principles taught, I was impressed with the familiarity of the problems presented and the clarity and simplicity of the solutions. I was especially impressed with the book's firm foundation in, and practical application of, gospel principles.

If you are like me, there are some tasks that seem insurmountable. Perhaps the monster of debt seems unconquerable, with no hope of liberation; yet, at the same time you have a desire to follow the commandments communicated through a living prophet. The principles taught in this book will help you on your way to slaying the giant that stands before you. These principles are built on a foundation of faith and honesty—honesty with the Lord, honesty with yourself, and honesty with your fellowman.

When Moses stood on the banks of the Red Sea with millions of Israelites, his task seemed impossible. Pharaoh and his army were advancing from behind, and the depths of the Red Sea were in front. There was no way known to man at that instant that he could accomplish what he had been commanded. But a way was revealed, and Moses took a leap of faith and "stretched out his hand over the sea" (Exodus 14:21). A way was prepared, the sea parted, the Israelites walked through on dry ground, and the sea swallowed the armies of Pharaoh.

On a smaller scale, Nephi and his brothers tried in vain to obtain the brass plates from Laban. They tried all they knew to do but were unsuccessful. Nephi still had a desire to fulfill the Lord's commands, but he didn't know how. He too took a leap of faith and returned to Jerusalem "not knowing beforehand the things which [he] should do" (1 Nephi 4:6). Again the Lord prepared a way to accomplish the impossible.

The prophet Ether taught that the witness (which could also be called the *blessing*) comes only after a trial of faith—faith that is manifest by your actions. The principles taught in this book will teach you the steps to take as you exercise your faith in the Lord Jesus Christ and follow the admonitions and commandments of modern-day prophets to get your house in order.

To the Lord, all things are spiritual. The Lord's laws dealing with finances are inseparably connected with the principle of tithing. The prophet Malachi asks the question, "Will a man rob God?" (Malachi 3:8). Then he proceeds to clarify by stating, "Yet ye have robbed me. But ye say, wherein have we robbed thee? In tithes and offerings. Ye are cursed with a curse: for ye have robbed me, even this whole nation. Bring ye all the tithes into the store-house, that there may be meat in mine house, and prove me now herewith, saith the Lord of hosts, if I will not open you the windows of heaven, and pour you out a blessing, that there shall not be room enough to receive it" (Malachi 3:8–10).

In the Doctrine and Covenants 130:20–21 we are taught, "There is a law, irrevocably decreed in heaven before the foundations of this world, upon which all blessings are predicated—and when we obtain any blessing from God, it is by obedience to that law upon which it is predicated." If we are to receive the outpouring of blessings promised by Malachi, we must pay our tithing first to the Lord. If we are honest with the Lord, and give back to Him the tenth of what He has given to us with a willing and cheerful heart, He will bless us in our endeavors to slay the monster of debt that plagues us in these latter days.

The Doctrine and Covenants further teaches, "I, the Lord, am bound when ye do what I say; but when ye do not what I say, ye have no promise" (82:10).

I have seen in my own life, as well as in the lives of others, the blessings that come when tithes are cheerfully and faithfully paid first—even when it appears to be an impossible request. Throughout this book the authors speak of living within your means and paying your debts as quickly as possible. These principles have been tried and tested repeatedly, and have been proven to be effective. The effectiveness of the principles is enhanced by being completely honest with the Lord and paying a full tithing. His promises are sure and will be fulfilled as you, like Moses and Nephi before you, exercise your faith in Him.

The principles in this book are also built on the foundation of honesty with yourself. It has been said that one definition of insanity is to do the same thing as always but expect different results. Before you can truly make progress in the elimination of debt, you have to honestly assess your situation and recognize that there is a problem. This can be a difficult self-assessment, but it is necessary in order to build up the motivation to try something different.

Finally, honesty with the Lord and yourself is accompanied by honesty with your fellowman. King David in the thirty-seventh Psalm explains "The wicked borroweth, and payeth not again" (Psalm 37:21). The shell game of debt transfers to different vehicles (for example, transferring a balance from one low-interest-rate credit card to another) will only defer the inevitable. In fact, this game can ultimately damage your ability to accomplish the Lord's designs, because as your available credit continues to grow, the temptation to incur more debt may become irresistible.

The principles set forth in this book are effective. Their effectiveness is enhanced as we exercise our faith and are honest with the Lord, ourselves, and our fellowman. I hope the tools presented in this book will bring freedom from the bondage of debt to all who implement them. All things are possible to those who place their faith in our Savior Jesus Christ and follow His commandments.

—Kraig Kuttler
CPA, MBA

Preface

In the October 1998 priesthood session of general conference, President Gordon B. Hinckley issued a wake-up call to the members of the Church. After retelling the account of Pharaoh's dream in the days of Joseph of old, he warned the Church:

> Now, brethren, I want to make it very clear that I am not prophesying, that I am not predicting years of famine in the future. But I am suggesting that the time has come to get our houses in order.
>
> So many of our people are living on the very edge of their incomes. In fact, some are living on borrowings. . . .
>
> . . . I am troubled by the huge consumer installment debt which hangs over the people of the nation, including our own people. In March 1997 that debt totaled $1.2 trillion, which represented a 7 percent increase over the previous year. . . .
>
> I recognize that it may be necessary to borrow to get a home, of course. But let us buy a home that we can afford and thus ease the payments which will constantly hang over our heads without mercy or respite for as long as 30 years. . . .
>
> Since the beginnings of the Church, the Lord has spoken on this matter of debt. To Martin Harris through revelation, He said: "Pay the debt thou hast contracted with the printer. Release thyself from bondage" (D&C 19:35). . . .
>
> What a wonderful feeling it is to be free of debt, to have a

little money against a day of emergency put away where it can be retrieved when necessary.

President Faust would not tell you this himself. Perhaps I can tell it, and he can take it out on me afterward. He had a mortgage on his home drawing 4 percent interest. Many people would have told him he was foolish to pay off that mortgage when it carried so low a rate of interest. But the first opportunity he had to acquire some means, he and his wife determined they would pay off their mortgage. He has been free of debt since that day. That's why he wears a smile on his face, and that's why he *whistles while he works.*

I urge you, brethren, to look to the condition of your finances. I urge you to be modest in your expenditures, discipline yourselves in your purchases to avoid debt to the extent possible. *Pay off debt as quickly as you can, and free yourselves from bondage.* ("To the Boys and to the Men," *Ensign,* November 1998, 52–53; emphasis added.)

From the moment that talk was given, you and I probably felt an urgency to do something about conquering our debt and controlling our finances. Yet so many of us feel that being debt-free is an overwhelming and near-impossible task. Where do we begin? How do we do this? Is being free from debt possible? Perhaps, from that day to the present, you have been earnestly endeavoring to live the counsel of the prophet, yet you are continually discouraged as the ups and downs of life are keeping your goal constantly just beyond your reach. If this describes your feelings, then this book was written for you.

We hope that this handbook—complete with worksheets and easy-to-use computer software to guide even the novice through the often-confusing maze of family finance—will offer each reader the peace and tranquility the prophet desires for us. We hope you will learn from it and soon "whistle while you work!"

—Lyle and Tracy Shamo

CHAPTER 1

Making a Case Against Debt

In the time of prosperity, get out of debt. . . . If you desire to prosper, and to be . . . a free people, first meet your obligations to God, and then . . . to your fellowmen.

—Joseph F. Smith

Money! There's a word no one can feel neutral about. There's no denying that the pursuit of money, even if it is just to feed and clothe our families and put a roof over our heads, consumes more of our time than eating, drinking, or spending time with family. Whether we love it or hate it, acquiring money is an indispensable part of modern life.

The problem is that, for most of us, there is just simply not enough money to go around. If you often find yourself living from paycheck to paycheck with little left over for any unexpected expenses, then you're among the norm. That's why even the smallest setback can send so many of us into a near panic.

Even more, our society has created a near fixation on material things and the amassing of wealth. The temptation has become so great that many of us have been drawn into it, even unawares. So much so that President Spencer W. Kimball was moved to warn the Church:

"The Lord has blessed us as a people with a prosperity unequaled in times past. The resources that have been placed in our power are good, and necessary to our work here on the earth. But I am afraid that many of us have been surfeited with flocks and herds and acres and barns and wealth and have begun to worship them as false gods, and they have power over us. Do we have more of these good things than our faith can stand? Many people spend most of their time working in the service of a self-image that includes sufficient money, stocks, bonds, investment portfolios, property, credit cards, furnishings, automobiles, and the like to guarantee carnal security throughout, it is hoped, a long and happy life. Forgotten is the fact that our assignment is to use these many resources in our families and quorums to build up the kingdom of God" ("The False Gods We Worship," *Ensign,* June 1976, 4).

In short, money, of necessity, may be the means to many of life's greatest opportunities; but it almost never forms the substance of our happiness. In a speech designed to offer "observations about the constant and fundamental principles which, if followed, will bring financial security and peace of mind under *any* economic circumstances," President N. Eldon Tanner quoted from the famed Norwegian playwright Henrik Ibsen: "Money may be the husk of many things, but not the kernel. It brings you food, but not appetite; medicine, but not health; acquaintances, but not friends; servants, but not faithfulness; days of joy, but not peace or happiness" (quoted in "Constancy Amid Change," *Ensign,* November 1979, 80).

We live in a society where we are dependent on money and what money can buy. Whether we are blinded by a worldly philosophy of money management, enticed by slick advertisers, mired in circumstances beyond our control, or lack the proper knowledge and skills to improve our financial situation, most of us find ourselves just getting by until disaster strikes. Then, like all too many Americans, we find ourselves unable to meet even the basic needs of our family. Like it or not, meeting basic needs has nothing to do with poverty and everything to do with how well we manage our money.

The following article, written after the United States Census Bureau released a report on Americans' ability to meet basic financial needs, illustrates this fact:

> About *one-fifth of all Americans* (nearly 48.6 million persons) lived in households that *had at least one difficulty in meeting basic needs.* This included not paying utility bills, not paying mortgage or rent, needing to see a doctor or dentist but not going, having telephone or utility service shut off, being evicted, not getting enough to eat, or otherwise not meeting essential expenses. . . .
>
> One would expect that persons with the lowest incomes would be the most likely to experience problems. . . .
>
> However, . . . 8.1 million persons . . . earning more than $45,700 per year . . . at some point during the year could not meet basic needs. . . . It appears that many persons did not manage their resources particularly well—failing to control expenditures, getting too far into debt, or neglecting to have reserves on which they could rely in times of emergency. . . .
>
> This 1995 study also found that more than one-fourth of all children in the U.S. lived in a household that had at least one difficulty meeting basic needs. (In "Meeting Basic Needs in America," *Information Center News* [newsletter] July 19, 1999, vol. 9, no. 11, 1–2.)

America—"the land of the free and the home of the brave"—has become a nation in debt. In July 2001, the Lutheran Brotherhood published a survey which discovered that a full 40 percent of all Americans admitted to living beyond their means, while 46 percent noted their debt was either increasing or staying the same each month. In short, nearly half of all Americans were unable to pay down their burden of debt. As if this wasn't bad enough, the second finding of this survey was even more sobering. "Because of their burden of debt, 22 percent of respondents admitted that they had to postpone buying necessities for their families" (In "American Style Debt," *Information Center News*, December 21, 2001, vol. 11, no. 20, 2).

Debt is not a new phenomenon in this country. We define ourselves in our society not by title but by the things we own. A successful person has a nice car, a nice house, nice furnishings, and owns any number of successful accouterments such as recreational vehicles, boats, or vacation property. They go on cruises, buy lavish presents for their friends, and dress to the nines.

Attempting to appear successful but lacking adequate resources, many people resort to debt. In a long-forgotten age, debtors were imprisoned. How grateful we are that we have come a long way since then. Even in our present day, however, debt is still a prison with bars made not of steel but of fear, worry, sleepless nights, and with relentless and abusive calls of creditors.

The urbanization and de-personalization of American society has made acquiring debt all too easy. Just a century ago, buying on installment meant borrowing from the sewing machine shop owner or the piano maker or the auto dealer—people you knew personally. In those days most of us would not have dreamed of missing a payment because we knew our creditors. We knew their families and their circumstances and we longed to maintain our respectability. Today our creditors are nameless, faceless people with addresses very often hundreds, perhaps thousands, of miles away. The stigma associated with not being able to pay a creditor is dissolved.

Along with this de-personalization came the advent of the

credit card. While thirty years ago credit card use was scarce, today few do not possess a credit card. Credit cards enable us to have capital available whenever or wherever the need arises for business expenses, travel, emergencies, and even for necessities. But it has its perils. Along with the consumer credit card came a household debt ratio that has soared off the charts. In the nineties alone, consumer debt soared a whopping 123 percent, and today one in every forty households files for bankruptcy protection each year. Americans owe $700 billion in installment debt, most of which is owed to credit cards. That is about $10,000 for each family and that amount does not include debt for mortgages or for automobile loans (see Paul J. Lim and Matthew Benjamin, "Digging Your Way Out of Debt," *U.S. News & World Report*, March 19, 2001, 52–60).

In an exposé on American debt, *US News & World Report* nailed the debt problem in this country on the head:

"Part of the problem with our debt obsession is that, for some, it is close to an addiction. Managing debt isn't like controlling most other compulsions. If you're a drinker, you can keep alcohol out of your house. If you're a gambler, you can avoid the weekend trips to Vegas. But if you're a chronic debtor, you don't have to do anything to fall over the precipice because the precipice often comes to you, especially during economic downturns" (Lim, "Digging Your Way Out of Debt," 57).

The evils of debt are not unknown to you. We don't need to convince you. If you've bought this book, then you are convinced that something must be done to reverse the cycle of debt. What you want to know is "How do I fix it?" The purpose of this book is to provide principles that will allow you to, in Elder Marvin J. Ashton's words, "Manage [your] money before it manages you" ("One for the Money," *Ensign*, July 1975, 72).

The sum and substance of the message of the gospel when it comes to matters of personal finance has been unalterable, steady, and true. It is summed up in President Gordon B. Hinckley's remarks at the priesthood session of general conference in October 1998. It is: "Be modest in your expenditures; discipline yourselves in your purchases to avoid debt to the extent possible. Pay off debt as quickly as you can.

" . . . have a reserve, even though it be small, then should storms howl about your head, you will have shelter for your wives and children and peace in your hearts" ("To the Boys and to the Men," *Ensign,* November 1998, 53). The principles taught within these pages adhere to gospel principles. The methods we describe are not new, and the knowledge we offer is not unique, but we can offer hope and peace in matters of money. Our message is simple: You can be in charge, you can be the conqueror, you can be debt free and secure no matter the size of your paycheck.

CHAPTER 2

Freedom from Debt— A Beginning

Get out of debt and rid yourself of the terrible bondage that debt brings.

—Gordon B. Hinckley

Ken and Terri were young, married, and in their early thirties. For the first years of their ten-year marriage, Ken went to school. Times were tough and student loans were a necessity. As they saw it, education debt was more of an investment than a liability. They looked upon their first mortgage the same way. They purchased their little home shortly after Ken's graduation. In quick succession came surprises and sometimes financial reverses. The burden of debt began to mount. There were cars, medical emergencies, a bout of unemployment, and the addition of three children—all of which placed tremendous strain on their pocketbook. Their initial goal was to always live within their means. They knew that to be a principle of the gospel. They tried to live up to their goal, but the challenges of life left them with a discouraging burden of debt.

When President Gordon B. Hinckley urged Church members to get out of debt, Terri felt overwhelmed and discouraged. She ran to her mother in tears. "Mom," she sobbed, "I've always tried to be obedient. I want to be obedient now. But how do I do it? I've tried but I just can't do it. It seems that whenever we are able to get a little ahead, some crisis or another comes along, and we fall deeper into debt. Is there no escape? Can I ever get out of debt?"

"Why, honey," sympathized Terri's mother, "It's not impossible, and you can do it! You just need to learn how."

Terri's mother was right. You know this. You know it instinctively. Whatever the Lord asks is never impossible. It may not always be easy, but with a little know-how, a sprinkle of elbow grease, a smattering of patience, and a great deal of faith you can conquer your debts and weather the financial storms that come your way.

The problem is that for most of us, even though our trust in the Lord is infinite, our trust in ourselves is a little shaky. Have you ever left a church meeting thoroughly discouraged after a discussion of finances? You are not alone. Perhaps you even muttered to yourself: "Pay off my debts? Hah! I might as well have been told to eat an elephant."

It's a good analogy. An old joke began with the question, "How do you eat an elephant? And the answer was, "One bite at a time." The question and the answer are not necessarily humorous because enormous undertakings are always successfully executed one step at a time. Debt is conquered in exactly the same way.

The road that leads from debt takes us to a brighter future where dreams become reality. That road may not be a super-highway, and the vehicle we travel in will probably not be a grand prix race car; but the path is sure and the destination not nearly as distant as it might seem. One day, for you and your family, debt will be only an unpleasant memory.

What Is Debt?

To read the map toward our destination, we must gain an understanding of a few terms. What is debt? Despite the efforts of today's society to confuse us, *debt* is still any bill that is overdue or requires more than one month to complete payment. Debt is the rental of money. Is credit different than debt? No, *credit* is not different from debt. Credit is a name invented by a slick advertising establishment. It carries none of the negative connotations of debt, but nonetheless it is, in reality, just plain, old debt.

Debt always carries with it a companion. We call that companion *interest*.

The biggest problem associated with debt is that the interest is always accumulating. That makes debt an ever-constant drain on your pocketbook. It wastes your hard-earned dollars, and it limits your freedom to choose how to spend your money. Benjamin Franklin correctly warned the people of his day: "Think what you do when you run in debt; you give to another power over your liberty" (quoted in Ezra Taft Benson, "Pay Thy Debt, and Live," *Ensign*, June 1987, 3).

Debt used to carry just those negative connotations, but advertising has changed all that. Years of fast-paced and enticing ads have obscured the obvious and replaced an aversion to debt with an "I need it now" attitude. No wonder *US News & World Report* reported in a June 8, 1987 issue: "The old virtues of scrimping and saving have been replaced with plastic gratification—thanks to the credit card" (Jack Egan, "Sizing Up Your Finances," 52).

We have fallen into a trap—a trap of ease and credit driven by our desires to keep up with our neighbors.

Leaders of the Church from every age have warned members about the pernicious influence of debt. Just over a hundred years ago, President Joseph F. Smith urged:

"In the time of prosperity, which we are now enjoying, it is highly proper for the Latter-day Saints to get out of debt. . . . Wherever I have had the opportunity of speaking, I have scarcely ever forgotten to hold out to the people the necessity . . . of our settling our obligations and freeing ourselves from debt in the day of prosperity" (*Gospel Doctrine* [Salt Lake City: Deseret Book, 1939], 259).

Some twenty years later, President Smith's admonition was followed by this from President Heber J. Grant: "Right here let me warn the Latter-day Saints to buy automobiles and to buy the ordinary necessities of life when they have the money to buy them, and not to mortgage their future." On another occasion he reminded the Saints: "There is a peace and a contentment which comes into the heart when we live within our means. There is no question about it" (*Gospel Standards*, comp. G. Homer Durham [Salt Lake City: Improvement Era, 1944], 111).

In our own day, President Howard W. Hunter issued these admonitions: "Latter-day Saints have always been known as a frugal people; it is part of our history. We have been conservative in our actions and we have lived within our means, but what goes on about us often encourages us to live beyond our means and incur debt. . . . One of the greatest burdens we have had placed upon us and the thing that has taken more of our freedom than any other, perhaps, is indebtedness" (*The Teachings of Howard W. Hunter*, comp. Clyde J. Williams [Salt Lake City: Bookcraft, 1997], 159).

"Do not covet what you have or what you do not have. . . . Things eventually work out financially; hang on and have faith" (*Teachings*, 162).

"This is a materialistic world, and Latter-day Saints must be careful not to confuse luxuries with necessities. . . . There are some who unwisely aspire to self-indulgent luxuries that often lead them away from complete commitment to the gospel of our Savior" (*Teachings*, 162).

Credit and her twin sister, debt, have been hanging around for many years. The peril of their influence has never diminished. Read carefully the counsel given by President Ezra Taft Benson:

> Our inspired leaders have always urged us to get out of debt, live within our means, and pay as we go. . . .
>
> Many people do not believe that serious recession will ever come again. Feeling secure in their expectations of continuing employment and a steady flow of wages and salaries, they obligate their future income without thought of what they would do if they should lose their jobs or if their incomes were stopped for some other reason. But the best authorities have repeatedly said that we are not yet smart enough to control our economy without downward adjustments. Sooner or later these adjustments will come.
>
> Another reason for increase in debt is even deeper and causes greater concern. This is the rise of materialism, as contrasted with commitment to spiritual values. Many a family, in order to make a "proper showing," will commit itself for a larger and more expensive house than is needed, in an expensive neighborhood. Almost everyone would, it seems, like to keep up with the Joneses. With the rising standard of living, that temptation increases with each new gadget that comes on the market. The subtle, carefully planned techniques of modern advertising are aimed at the weakest points of consumer resistance. As a result, there is a growing feeling, unfortunately, that material things should be had now, without waiting, without saving, without self-denial. ("Pay Thy Debt and Live," *Ensign*, June 1987, 3–4.)

Debt is a major problem in American society. According to a 2001 Associated Press article, "Americans are spending 14.3 percent of their take-home pay on debts. . . . Credit card delinquencies—accounts at least 30 days past due—have been hovering at about 5 percent. . . . [And] mortgage delinquencies rose to 4.5 percent of outstanding loans in the final quarter of 2000" (Eileen

Alt Powell, "Consumer Debt Higher Than Ever," *South Bend Tribune*, June 20, 2001, B8).

The article reported that "Durant Abernathy, president of the National Foundation for Credit Counseling, a nonprofit organization that helps families with debt problems, said that the number of people seeking assistance is rising rapidly.

"'Our average client—the policeman, the firefighter, the teacher, the nurse—is carrying more debt than they've ever carried, and they're in trouble,' Abernathy said. 'If their overtime is cut back or a husband or wife is laid off, they have virtually no savings, so they go over the edge'" (ibid.).

Obviously, being out of debt grants us many more options than remaining in debt. But are there times when we have no other viable option?

Good Debt

Is there ever such a thing as good debt? Yes. Not all debt is bad. Elder Ezra Taft Benson agreed that "sound business debt and reasonable debt for education are elements of growth. Sound mortgage credit is a real help to a family that must borrow for a home." But, as always, he adds a caveat: "If you must incur debt to meet the reasonable necessities of life—such as buying a house and furniture—then, I implore you to value your solvency and happiness, buy within your means. So use credit wisely—to acquire an education, a farm, [or] to own a home" ("The Dangerous Threat of Increasing Indebtedness," *The Instructor*, May 1962, 159, 162).

President Benson knew that despite the soundness and wellbeing that comes from acquiring a home, an education, or a new business, there is still risk involved. To avoid that risk we must plan in advance to pay off any debts as quickly as it is possible, and we must force ourselves to borrow only that which we can reasonably afford.

Bad Debt

Bad debt is much more plentiful. We all know what bad debt is. It includes borrowing for fleeting impulses. Purchasing things that we think we want but we really don't need and we can't hope to pay for. These are material things—things like clothes, vacations, and expensive dinners. All of us are guilty at times of spending money to buy things we can't afford to impress people who don't care.

Interest

We've already talked a little about interest, but let's explore it more thoroughly. All debt—good or bad—comes with a price tag. Let's explain. When a person applies for a loan he borrows the amount he needs to cover his expenses. The money you receive or are actually advanced by a financial institution (such as the bank, credit union, savings and loan, department store, or credit card company) is called the *principal*. The principal of the loan is the actual amount that you borrow.

Financial institutions are not service agencies. They cannot remain in business unless they make a profit. They are not mean, ugly monsters. It's a matter of simple economics. They have to charge you something to pay their own bills. Therefore, your bank or credit card company charges you a fee for renting their money. This fee is called *interest*. Interest is calculated on a percentage of the principal. That percentage is how your lender makes his profit.

Interest is computed on an annual basis and is included in your *monthly payment*. The monthly payment pays the lender back both principal and interest. Some loans are set up so that you pay the bulk of the interest at the beginning of your loan period. This ensures that your lender will receive his profit. This isn't a rip-off; it's just good business.

Payments are spread over a specified period of time—this is called the *term* of the loan. For example, auto loans are made generally, in three- to five-year terms, while home mortgages can extend over a fifteen- to thirty-year term. Some loans do not have a term; they charge an *annual percentage rate* (APR) of interest until the balance is paid in full.

Some loans, such as a mortgage loan, require a schedule for your monthly payments. That schedule tells you, the borrower, how much of each payment goes toward paying off the principal and how much goes toward paying off the interest. This is called an *amortization table*. As you follow an amortization table you will see that at the very beginning of your payment period, your monthly payment pays almost all interest and very little principal. Gradually, as you follow through the amortization table, the amount of interest lessens, while the amount of principal increases. Halfway through the term of your loan, you will pay half your monthly payment to principal and half to interest. At the end of the term, you will pay nearly all the monthly payment toward the principal. If you have been paying on a loan for several years, you may need to have an amortization table to determine the amount of principal you still owe.

When it comes time to compute real debt, include both the principal and the interest. That is because, whether you like it or not, creditors will not forgive your debts until you have paid them both. If you make payments on time and never try to speed up the process, by the end of the term on your loan, you would have expended roughly three and one-half times the original principal. What a waste of good money!

Elder Marvin J. Ashton of the Quorum of the Twelve spoke no

truer words than these: "It is a happy day financially when time and interest are working for you and not against you" ("One for the Money," *Ensign*, July 1975, 73). Those who understand interest collect it. Those who do not, pay it. President J. Reuben Clark offered us the clearest visual image of the pernicious nature of interest:

> Interest never sleeps nor sickens nor dies; it never goes to the hospital; it works on Sundays and holidays; it never takes a vacation; it never visits nor travels; it takes no pleasure; it is never laid off work nor discharged from employment; it never works on reduced hours; it never has short crops nor droughts; it never pays taxes; it buys no food, it wears no clothes; it is unhoused and without home and so has no repairs, no replacements, no shingling, plumbing, painting, or whitewashing; it has neither wife, children, father, mother, nor kinfolk to watch over and care for; it has no expense of living; it has neither weddings nor births nor deaths; it has no love, no sympathy, it is as hard and soulless as a granite cliff. Once in debt, interest is your companion every minute of the day and night; you cannot shun it or slip away from it; you cannot dismiss it; it yields neither to entreaties, demands, or orders; and whenever you get in its way or cross its course or fail to meet its demands, it crushes you. (In Conference Report, April 1938, 103.)

Debt Management Rules

As you begin your commitment to be debt-free, we suggest setting eight simple rules:

1. I will not incur any additional debt.
2. From this day forward I will pay as I go.
3. I will pay off my debt as quickly as possible to avoid paying huge interest payments.
4. I will avoid impulse buying and I will plan for every penny I spend. (This will ensure that you will have the money necessary to pay your debts.)

5. I will budget carefully and find extra money to apply against my existing debt.
6. I will remain committed to being free from debt for the rest of my life.
7. Once free from debt, I will develop a savings account for future purchases.
8. I will manage my funds, and I will no longer allow them to manage me.

Freedom from debt

We want to end this chapter on a high note. When debts are gone, your dreams can become reality. What are your dreams? Do you want a college education for your children? Do you want to pay for your children's missions? Would you like to have a little nest egg to help your married children when they face hard times? Do you want to retire and serve your own mission? Perhaps you dream of a whole string of missions to take you through your sunset years? Perhaps you've always dreamed of standing on a sunlit beach and feeling the cool seawater beneath your toes, or maybe you'd like to travel the oceans wide and discover the world? Any dream you plan for can become your reality no matter what your income level. But it begins by earning interest instead of paying it.

You can be rich. Rich is feeling the wind against your face and not feeling afraid. Rich is having the peace of mind that you are prepared. Rich is feeling that it is good to be alive. It is the kind of richness described by a wise and dear friend: "As my husband and I got out of debt, we found ourselves focusing less on material things and focusing more on the things that matter most."

Isn't this what life is really about? Wouldn't it be nice to have the time and energy to devote to the things which matter most to you? You can find freedom from the bondage of debt.

CHAPTER 3

How to Get Out of Debt

Self-reliance cannot be obtained when there is serious debt hanging over a household. One has neither independence nor freedom from bondage when he is obligated to others.
—GORDON B. HINCKLEY

There are varying degrees of indebtedness. Some people are living so close to the brink that they spend each day just trying to avoid their creditors and are desperate for any solution to their indebtedness. Some people are not particularly overwhelmed by their debt yet, but they are frustrated by living paycheck to paycheck and never getting ahead. These folks never seem to find sufficient funds to completely eliminate their debts. Some people aren't having immediate financial problems and their debt burden is relatively low compared to those around them, yet they fear a financial reversal because they suspect it could cause them serious problems. And, of course, there are those few people who earn so much money that they never worry about debt. They are secure and they know that whatever circumstance they find themselves in, there are always finances sufficient to bail themselves out. This last group is so rare that it may, perhaps, even be nonexistent. No matter the size of our paychecks, most of us seem to carry a burden of debt.

Determining Your Debt-to-Income Ratio

How much debt is too much? Like everything else, that can be determined only on an individual basis. For some, $2,000 is too much debt; while for others the burden could run as high as $100,000 or even higher. A common tool to determine whether your debt is unreasonably high is referred to as the *debt-to-income ratio*. This is a mathematical calculation that compares your total debt to your total income. If you divide the amount you owe by the amount you make each year, and then multiply that quotient by 100, you arrive at your ratio. For example, if Meg makes $80,000 a year and has a monthly debt payment of $2,500, she has a debt ratio of 37.5 percent. Generally speaking, if you pay more than 35 percent of your income to debt, then you ought to do something about it. You are in trouble. What is your debt-to-income ratio?

$$\frac{\text{total annual debt payments}}{\text{annual income}} \quad x \ 100 = \text{Debt-to-Income Ratio}$$

Pulling yourself out of debt can be achieved by implementing a variety of options. We'll discuss most of them. Which you choose will depend entirely on your circumstances and the degree of your indebtedness. We'll start our discussion of these various options by demonstrating the simplest and easiest solution for most families to pay down their debts.

There is a step-by-step process for getting out of debt. Each step builds momentum for the next. The first step to freedom from debt will be to fill out the computer worksheets provided on the disk that comes with this book. Once you fill out the worksheets, your computer will automatically calculate your debts and work to prepare you for each additional step in the process of becoming debt-free. If you don't have Microsoft Excel® and cannot read the files on the disk, you can use the PDF images of each worksheet and figure the calculations with a business or financial calculator (these calculators are available for free downloading on most bank and credit union web sites).

As a side note: The key to success in debt elimination is to *involve your family in the process.* Husbands and wives must work together as they fill out the worksheets. Perhaps your arrangement is that one or the other of you worries about the finances and the other just "goes along." To eliminate debt, this will not work. To become debt-free requires united effort. By designating only one-half of a critical partnership to this primary responsibility, the family is vulnerable to failure and invites money squabbles into the relationship.

Additionally, older children can and ought to be included in discussions about family financial goals. You'll probably be pleasantly surprised at the enthusiasm your children will generate in this process. They can assist you in reaching your goals. This will be particularly true when you paint a vision of how exciting it will be when family dreams are realized.

Of course, not everyone is married. If you live alone then you make all your own financial decisions, which, in some respects, makes the process of getting out of debt simpler. However, if you need advice or help, don't discount turning to your extended family—your mother and father or your brothers and sisters—for help. Part of Heavenly Father's plan for families is that we support each other in all things.

Debt Elimination: A Three-Step Process

The process we outline in this book and on the CD-ROM is very simple and can be accomplished in three steps:

Step 1: Identification of Debts. This step will show you exactly where you are with your debts by helping you create a complete list of debts and their interest rates, monthly payments, balances due, and remaining number of payments on each.

Step 2: How Far Are You Really in Debt? Completing this step will show you how much you are going to pay in interest in addition to the principal of the debt. To calculate this, multiply the number of payments due by the monthly payment.

Step 3: How Long for Payoff? This is the most important step of the process. It shows you how quickly your debts will disappear and how long it will be before you are free from debt forever!

Identification of Debts

The rest of this chapter will teach you how to fill out the worksheets provided on the CD-ROM. As you read, you'll need to examine each worksheet individually to help you visualize the process. To use the computerized worksheets, place the CD-ROM in the appropriate drive on your computer. Follow the on-screen instructions to install the program on your hard drive. Whenever you want to work on your debt-elimination plan, click on the Debt-Free folder and start the program. All worksheets are accessible through the main menu.

Step 1—Identification of Debts—can be completed using the Debt Elimination Worksheet. To access this worksheet, go to the main menu on the CD-ROM and click the button that says Begin the three-step debt elimination process. (A blank worksheet is also on pages 40–41). List your debts in any order you choose. The program will later reorder them to show you how to pay them off. If you are doing the worksheet by hand, list your debts from the smallest amount owed to the largest amount owed. Remember this definition: *Debt is any bill that is overdue or requires more than one month to complete payment.* Do not confuse debt with cost-of-living expenses, such as rent or utilities.

Some debt-elimination programs require that you rank your loans by interest rate, beginning with the largest percentage rate and moving to the smallest. Some believe there is an advantage to paying off the highest interest-bearing loans first. However, the difference between tackling the highest interest-rate loans first versus tackling the shortest-term loan first is almost negligible. What is more, you can actually decrease the number of your debts faster by paying off the shortest-term loans first. (The computer program will reorder your debts to do this.) You will find greater personal satisfaction in seeing the number of your debts grow increasingly smaller.

If you are completing this worksheet by hand, the most difficult information to obtain will be the number of payments remaining. If you are using the computer spreadsheet, this number will be calculated automatically for you based on the interest rate, minimum payment, and balance you previously entered. For credit card debt, the number of payments remaining refers to the number of payments you would have to pay if you paid only the minimum payment each month and did not incur any additional debt. If you cannot calculate this amount based on any paperwork you have in your immediate possession, then call your lending institution and ask for it.

Example

For each worksheet we will illustrate the process by providing you with an example. That example is drawn from a fictional family we will call the Dixons. (Please note that the sample shown of Step 1 also includes the total determined in Step 2—How Far Are You Really in Debt?— We will get into those details later.)

Dan and Janet Dixon are an average family, with an average

DEBT ELIMINATION WORKSHEET

STEP 1 - IDENTIFICATION OF DEBTS

List _all_ debts, including your mortgage, credit cards, automobile, second mortgage, etc. Input information only in the green shaded cells.

TITLE	INT. RATE	MO. PAYMENT	BALANCE	_Approximate_ # OF PMTS REMAINING
Medical Doctor	0.00%	$ 25.00	$ 475.00	19.00
Orthodontist	0.00%	$ 62.50	$ 500.00	8.00
Credit Card A	19.90%	$ 25.02	$ 899.93	55.18
Credit Card B	21.00%	$ 74.22	$ 1,243.42	20.00
Credit Card C	16.50%	$ 75.50	$ 2,480.00	44.00
Home Equity Loan	9.90%	$ 77.00	$ 3,625.98	59.86
Auto Payment	7.90%	$ 202.00	$ 9,981.16	59.97
Mortgage	6.50%	$ 890.53	$ 137,440.00	334.65
TOTAL AMOUNT BORROWED			**$ 156,645.49**	

Note:
The approximate number of payments remaining can be identified in the following three ways:
1. Use the computer template titled "Debt Elimination Worksheet" that is included on the CD provided with this book. Enter the information requested; the payments will be calculated automatically.
2. Use any financial or business calculator that will calculate present value payments. Follow the instructions for your calculator to figure the number of payments.
3. Contact your creditor.

amount of children, earning an average income. Their burden of debt is likewise average in its nature. The Dixons are not in any way a real family, and the figures we assign to them are drawn for illustration purposes only. Let's introduce you to the Dixons now.

Dan Dixon has a middle-management position in a computer software company. Janet, his wife, works at home doing data entry. They are just two ordinary people trying to make their paychecks stretch and finding themselves sinking deeper into debt every year despite their best efforts. Their goal has always been to get out of debt "next year." But nothing goes right, and "next year" seems further and further away.

The Dixons smallest debt is the amount owed their doctor. It is $475, and the doctor is good enough to not charge them interest on it as long as the bill is paid on time every month. They pay $25 a month.

Their second smallest debt is to the orthodontist for their daughter Jamie's braces. They pay $62.50 a month to the orthodontist and owe $500 to pay it off in full.

Then come their credit cards. The smallest card has a balance of $899.93. They usually try to pay a little more than the minimum payment on all of their cards, yet when they calculated how long they'd be paying if they could make only the minimum payments, they were astounded to find that it would take four and a half years to pay off the first one in full—and that was only if they didn't add any additional debt.

The Dixons listed each debt. You can see the results in the example provided on the previous page. They ended the list with their auto loan and their mortgage.

How Far Are You Really in Debt?

After the Dixons listed all their debts, the computer software automatically calculated the amount of their real debt. This was

DEBT ELIMINATION WORKSHEET

STEP 2 - HOW FAR ARE YOU REALLY IN DEBT?

TITLE	INT. RATE	MO. PAYMENT [A]	BALANCE	Approximate # OF PMTS REMAINING [B]	Approximate LEVEL OF REAL DEBT [A] x [B]
Medical Doctor	0.00%	$ 25.00	$ 475.00	19.00	475.00
Orthodontist	0.00%	$ 62.50	$ 500.00	8.00	500.00
Credit Card A	19.90%	$ 25.02	$ 899.93	55.18	1,380.54
Credit Card B	21.00%	$ 74.22	$ 1,243.42	20.00	1,484.43
Credit Card C	16.50%	$ 75.50	$ 2,480.00	44.00	3,321.85
Home Equity Loan	9.90%	$ 77.00	$ 3,625.98	59.86	4,609.39
Auto Payment	7.90%	$ 202.00	$ 9,981.16	59.97	12,112.99
Mortgage	6.50%	$ 890.53	$ 137,440.00	334.65	298,012.68
TOTAL AMOUNT BORROWED			$ 156,645.49		$ 321,896.88

Note:
The level of real debt is calculated by multiplying the monthly payment **[A]** by the number of payments remaining on the debt **[B]**. This includes all principal and interest you will ultimately pay.

the sum of each monthly payment amount multiplied by the remaining number of payments. The sum represented the amount the Dixons would spend over the entire term of the debt if they made only the minimum payments each month. Of course, most people do not make only minimum payments over the term of their loans. In addition, most people never completely pay a debt in full before a new debt is incurred. For this reason, looking at real debt makes sense. Dollar for dollar, our illustration will be close to or even less than true amounts owed by people who never climb out of their indebtedness.

From our example worksheet, you can see that the Dixons have borrowed $156,645 in principal, but by the time they have paid off their existing loans, making only minimum payments each month, they will have actually expended $321,897 in real dollars. Does that leave you flabbergasted? It ought to. The difference between the principal and the principal-plus-interest is $165,252—that's considerably more than what they had originally borrowed. Can you believe it—$165,252 additional dollars—just for the rental of money!

This is the reason that debt is so ugly. It is the reason that those who understand interest collect it, those who do not understand interest pay it. Let's look at the gap between collecting interest through savings and paying it. We'll call it the interest gap.

The Interest Gap

-12%   0%   +6.5%

18.5%

18.5% x 10 years = 185%

When the interest rate gap is 18.5 percent, there is a 185

percent difference over ten years between collecting interest and paying it off in debts.

Let's look at that same gap another way. If the Dixons owe $156,645 in principal on all their debts, and are really in debt $321,897, then at the end of twenty-seven years, when the debts are fully paid, they would have lost $165,252.

But what if they could retire their debt far earlier and put the combined total of all those minimum payments toward savings and investments? In addition to being debt-free, in twenty-seven years they would have a tidy little nest egg to spend then on the realization of their dreams or anything that came along before that time could be realized as it was needed. Remember? Missions, weddings, travel, retirement, education—whatever the Dixons can dream of, they can make reality.

Now do you understand? Those who understand interest collect it, those who do not, pay it. So remain optimistic; wealth lies ahead for you as well—just as soon as you eliminate those debts.

Now comes the exciting part: Step 3—Determining How Long for Payoff. The next chapter will introduce you to the third step and the actual process of paying off your debts.

CHAPTER 4

The Power Payment Plan

Many more people could ride out the storm-tossed waves in their economic lives if they had their year's supply of food and clothing and were debt-free. Today we find that many have followed this counsel in reverse; they have at least a year's supply of debt and are food-free.

—THOMAS S. MONSON

A re you ready to kick that monster debt out of your house and home forever? Of course you are. You can do it without having to secure extra employment and without finding any additional sources of income. The power lies inside of you. It is so simple you will probably wonder why you never thought of it before. In fact, we predict that by the time you finish this chapter and have figured how long it will take you to pay off your debts, you will be so excited and energized that family finances will never look so discouraging again.

Every household, no matter the circumstances, wastes a certain amount of money each and every month, and that is the money you will use to get out of debt. In subsequent chapters we will spend a great deal of time discussing ways to find extra sources of money you did not even realize were available to you. But for now, you must accept on faith that it is likely that there is between 10 and 15 percent of your income that you can "break free" to "break the back of your debt." We'll call this money your *power payment*.

Here's how we'll start. At the beginning of next month, sit down with your family and make out a check for whatever amount of money you reasonably feel you can save from your monthly expenditures. This will be your power payment. (To find enough savings from your monthly expenses to make a power payment, be sure to check out the appendix, which lists a number of ways to cut expenses in every category of your budget—from heating bills to mortgage insurance, from entertainment to wardrobe needs.) You might consider writing out your power payment check immediately after writing out your tithing check. It only seems appropriate that after giving 10 percent to the Lord, that it is time to focus on the percent that will go to your debts. At the bottom of the power payment check, write in big letters: FOR PRINCIPAL ONLY. Make out your check at the beginning of the month so that you won't be tempted to spend it. Ideally, the amount of this check should be equal to the 10 percent to 15 percent that most experts agree the average household wastes each month. If this amount seems beyond your grasp, then make out a check for whatever amount you feel you can spare from your monthly spending plan, whether it be 3 percent or 7 percent or 10 percent. Any amount will get the ball rolling. However, we believe that as your spending becomes more efficient every month, you will eventually be able to reach at least 10 percent.

Now look at the current monthly statements sent by your creditors. You are going to make minimum monthly payments each month on all your debts except the debt you are currently concentrating on. This debt payment will include the regular check for the minimum monthly payment plus the power payment check. Continue to pay what you are paying right now. However, if the creditor requires you to increase a payment, then pay the increased amount. Never pay less but pay more if that is required. *Never fail to meet your obligations.*

When your payment becomes due, take the power payment check from its secure location. You didn't spend this money yet because you made out the check at the first of the month. Add this check to the second check and enclose it in the envelope for the monthly payment of your shortest debt as reordered on the Debt Elimination Worksheet. Pay this new amount until the shortest debt is paid in full. This should be a matter of just a few months or so—maybe less.

Let's go back to our sample family for just a moment so you can visualize how exciting it will be to see that first debt being wiped out. Remember, when we finished the last chapter, we ended with Step 2 on the Debt Elimination Worksheet. Now we move to Step 3. While the Dixons were completing steps 1 and 2 of the worksheet, they were also thinking about the amount of money they could afford to use as a power payment. They determined that they could come up with $425 a month, which is 10 percent of their monthly take-home pay. They entered that number in the box labeled "Initial Power Payment" on the worksheet, and the computer automatically calculated the "revised number of payments remaining" column for them. The computer also automatically renumbered their debts, putting the debt with the shortest pay-off time first. When the Dixons glanced at the computer calculation they were ecstatic. In just under ten years they would be debt-free. They weren't yet sure how this was going to work, but it made them feel good. They could hardly believe it! They quickly glanced down the chart and found that all those nagging debts—not including their mortgage payment—would be eliminated in just a couple of years. What a relief! Instead of a lifetime of debt, they were seeing

DEBT ELIMINATION WORKSHEET

STEP 3 - HOW LONG FOR PAYOFF?

INITIAL POWER PMT. = $ 425.00

Don't forget to put in your power payment as discussed in Chapter 4.

The debts are now listed in order of original payoff; the one that would naturally be paid off first is listed first and so on. Don't forget to enter your power payment as discussed in Chapter 4.

Reordered based on original payoff term

	TITLE	INT. RATE	MO. PAYMENT	BALANCE	ORIGINAL # OF PMTS REMAINING	(Approximate) REVISED # OF PMTS REMAINING
1	Orthodontist	0.00%	$ 62.50	$ 500.00	8.00	1.03
2	Medical Doctor	0.00%	$ 25.00	$ 475.00	19.00	1.88
3	Credit Card B	21.00%	$ 74.22	$ 1,243.42	20.00	3.90
4	Credit Card C	16.50%	$ 75.50	$ 2,480.00	44.00	7.51
5	Credit Card A	19.90%	$ 25.02	$ 899.93	55.18	8.72
6	Home Equity Loan	9.90%	$ 77.00	$ 3,625.98	59.86	13.01
7	Auto Payment	7.90%	$ 202.00	$ 9,981.16	59.97	21.70
8	Mortgage	6.50%	$ 890.53	$ 137,440.00	334.65	113.55

TOTAL NUMBER OF PAYMENTS: *(Months)* 113.55

DIVIDED BY 12 = *(Years)* 9.46

Note:
The numbers in the "approximate revised number of payments remaining" column are calculated on the worksheet found on the CD included with this book. The principle is based on the building block concept taught in the book, including a power payment. If you do not have a robust spreadsheet package, the same results can be obtained manually by following the principles taught in this book and manually calculating amortization schedules.

light at the end of the tunnel and they felt exhilaration. Becoming debt-free was within their grasp.

If you follow this plan, when your shortest debt is paid in full, you will be ready to concentrate on the next shortest debt. Your new power payment will be 10 percent of your take-home pay plus the minimum monthly payment of the first debt. With the elimination of each debt, the power payment will naturally grow larger. Each time, you will always begin by making out a check for the power payment and a second check for the minimum payment of the subsequent debt. Each time you pay a debt in full, you will add your original power payment to the sum of each debt that is now fully paid and then to the minimum payment of the next debt. By making additional payments on your principal you will pay less interest and more principal, thus accelerating the payment of your debt.

The whole process might be easier to visualize if you think of each debt as a stack of building blocks. Each of those blocks represents $100. Let us also assume that you have five debts—each, therefore, being represented by a building block and each debt carrying a minimum payment of $100. Your power payment is also equal to $100. Now, stack the power payment of $100 on top of the $100 minimum monthly payment of your lowest debt. You are now spending $200 toward the elimination of the first debt. When the first debt is eliminated, you will take the first two blocks, now representing $200, and stack them onto the next block. Now you are spending $300 toward the payment of the second debt. With the elimination of each debt, your power payment increases, and the momentum gathers. By the time you are ready to tackle the last of the five debts, you will have six $100 blocks stacked on top of each other and pay the entire $600 every month toward the last debt—$500 will be applied to the principal of the loan and $100 to both the principal and interest.

The Power Payment: Key to Success

Key to the success of this plan is that you always remember to send *two checks*—one being for principal only—to the creditor of whatever debt you are focusing on. Some who have tried this system before have found that their creditor becomes confused if they send one big check. This is because the creditor may assume you are paying minimum payments in advance, and the clerk recording your payment may not properly credit you. You need to ensure that your power payment pays only the principal of your debt.

Example

Let's show you how this works with real figures. We'll go back to our typical family, the Dixons. As you read our example, look at the chart titled "Power Payment Plan."

Dan and Janet's take-home pay totals $4,252 every month. This does not include taxes, social security, or insurance payments, which are deducted from their paychecks every pay period. Ten percent of that amount is $425. In the example chart that follows, this amount became their power payment.

At the beginning of the first month, Dan and Janet made out a power payment check for $425 to Dr. Simpson, their daughter's orthodontist. In the past, they had typically sent him a check for $62.50 every month; but that month they sent him two checks: one for $425 and the other for $62.50. In other words, they planned to send him $487.50. Since this debt did not include any interest, they did not need to make out two checks. However, if the business office had charged them interest, the first check, with "For Principal Only" written on it, would have alerted the business office that the Dixons wished to pay off their debt and that they were not making advance minimum payments, which would include both principal and interest. This may seem a little elementary. But sending two checks really helps to avoid confusion on the part of office employees. It also never hurts to follow up a power payment check with a phone call to see that the business office is properly crediting your principal payments. You'd be surprised how easy this seems and how confused some offices get. You are doing something most people don't do!

Because the balance of the Dixons's orthodontist bill was $500, their first debt was retired in just one month. Why? Because as soon as they realized they were within $12.50 of paying this first debt in full, they chipped in the extra money and included it in their second check. Next month, they planned to take the $425 power payment plus the $63 (rounded up from $62.50) they were accustomed to paying to the orthodontist and make out a new power payment check to Dr. Barton, their family doctor. Their new power payment would now total $488. They would then write out a check for $25, which was the minimum monthly payment for the doctor bill. They soon remembered, however, that they owed only $475 to the doctor. This meant that they could pay the second bill in full and have $38 left to add to their third debt, which was credit card B. In two months they were two debts shorter and on their way to paying off the third debt.

The third month enabled the Dixons to focus on their third debt. Their power payment was now $513 ($425+$63+$25—the minimum monthly payment for debt 2). When added to the minimum monthly payment of credit card B ($74.22, which we have rounded down to $74), the total payment going to the third debt became $587 per month. In just over three months, the debt from the orthodontist's bill, the doctor's bill and, credit card B was gone. With debts 1, 2, and 3 eliminated, Dan and Janet began focusing on the payment of the fourth debt (sending in one check

POWER PAYMENT PLAN—SAMPLE

INSTRUCTIONS:

Step 1: By careful budgeting, set aside 10 to 15 percent of your take-home pay.

Step 2: Apply the 10 to 15 percent toward the payment of debt 1. Make out a check for this amount. Write on the check "FOR PRINCIPAL ONLY" and apply it to debt 1. Write a second check for the regular monthly payment. Continue to make the regular monthly payment and the power payment for the remainder of your debts.

Step 3: When debt 1 is paid in full, make out a check for the 10 to 15 percent of your take-home pay plus the minimum monthly payment of debt 1. Apply this check toward the principal of debt 2. Make out a check for the regular monthly amount as well. Continue this procedure for each debt until all are paid in full.

Note: if you have more than 8 debts, simply make a copy of this template and place half of your debts on each.

$425 Power Payment (10 to 15 percent)

	Debt 1	Debt 2	Debt 3	Debt 4	Debt 5	Debt 6	Debt 7	Debt 8	Total Pmts
	$63	$25	$74	$76	$25	$77	$202	$891	$1,858
		$25	$74	$76	$25	$77	$202	$891	$1,858
			$74	$76	$25	$77	$202	$891	$1,858
				$76	$25	$77	$202	$891	$1,858

1

$425	
$63	Debt 1
$488	Until Debt 1 is paid off.

2

$425	
$63	
$25	Debt 2
$513	Until Debt 2 is paid off.

3

$425	
$63	
$25	
$74	Debt 3
$587	Until Debt 3 is paid off.

4

$425	
$63	
$25	
$74	
$76	Debt 4
$663	Until Debt 4 is paid off.

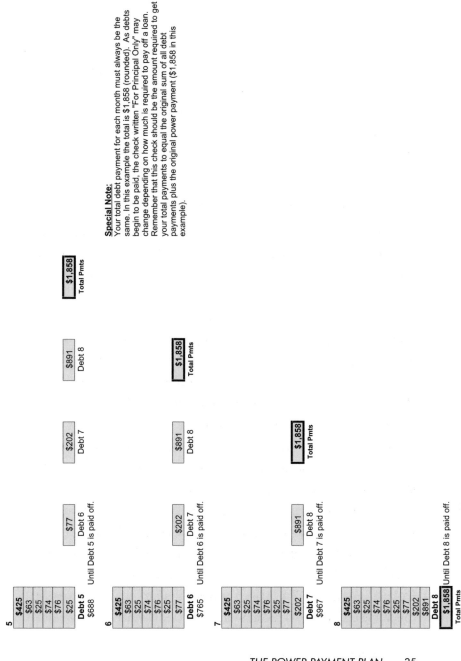

for $587 with "For principal only" written on it and a second check for the minimum monthly payment of credit card C—$76—every month). Dan and Janet continued to consolidate and roll down their debts until, in just under two years, all that remained was the mortgage on their house. Now, every month Dan writes out a power payment check for $967, and Janet writes "For principal only" in the corner of that check. Then Dan writes out the regular mortgage payment of $891, some of which goes to pay interest and some to principal. If they keep on schedule, in less than nine and one-half years, Dan and Janet will be totally out of debt.

Utilizing the Power Payment Plan

Now it's your turn to see how the Power Payment Plan will work for you. The program you installed will automatically make the mathematical calculations for you. For initial purposes, calculate 10 percent of your take-home pay and place that amount in the box entitled "Initial Power Payment" on the Debt Elimination Worksheet. (The box is found in Step 3 of the worksheet.) If you return to the Debt Elimination Menu on the CD-ROM and click the button that says See the "power" behind the Power Payment Plan, you'll see your own numbers formatted just like the chart on the previous page. This will allow you to see the extra amounts you will be placing toward each debt as you escalate its repayment. The sole purpose of that chart—the Power Payment Plan worksheet—is simply to give you an idea of how your power payment will escalate. To actually implement the Power Payment Program, you must follow the plan and write out that monthly power payment check. Soon, like the Dixons, you'll be able to see your way to becoming debt-free. If you need to, you can always return to the Debt Elimination Worksheet and recalculate your repayment timetable according to the amount of power payment you are able to comfortably make. Any amount will pay off your debts faster than you are currently doing; likewise, any amount will get that ball rolling.

Does this seem unbelievable? Test it for yourself. We warn you: The system we are teaching you is the same system many debt-relief companies use to pay down your debt—and they charge you good money to do it. But you can do it for yourself. Test it. See how easy it is for you to kick debt out of your life.

DEBT ELIMINATION WORKSHEET—SAMPLE

STEP 1 - IDENTIFICATION OF DEBTS

*List **all** debts, including your mortgage, credit cards, automobile, second mortgage, etc. Input information only in the green shaded cells.*

	TITLE	INT. RATE	MO. PAYMENT	BALANCE	Approximate # OF PMTS REMAINING	Approximate LEVEL OF REAL DEBT
2	Medical Doctor	0.00%	$ 25.00	$ 475.00	19.00	475.00
1	Orthodontist	0.00%	$ 62.50	$ 500.00	8.00	500.00
5	Credit Card A	19.90%	$ 25.02	$ 899.93	55.18	1,380.54
3	Credit Card B	21.00%	$ 74.22	$ 1,243.42	20.00	1,484.43
4	Credit Card C	16.50%	$ 75.50	$ 2,480.00	44.00	3,321.85
6	Home Equity Loan	9.90%	$ 77.00	$ 3,625.98	59.86	4,609.39
7	Auto Payment	7.90%	$ 202.00	$ 9,981.16	59.97	12,112.99
8	Mortgage	6.50%	$ 890.53	$ 137,440.00	334.65	298,012.68
						–
						–
						–
						–
						–
						–
						–
						–
						–
						–
	TOTAL AMOUNT BORROWED			**$ 156,645.49**		**$ 321,896.88**

STEP 2 - HOW FAR ARE YOU REALLY IN DEBT? $ 321,896.88

This number is calculated by multiplying each monthly payment by the remaining number of payments for that debt, then adding all of the resulting amounts as shown above.

STEP 3 - HOW LONG FOR PAYOFF?

POWER PMT. = $ 425.00

Don't forget to put in your power payment as discussed in Chapter 4.

The debts are listed in order of original payoff; the one that would naturally be paid off first is listed first and so on. Don't forget to enter your power payment as discussed in Chapter 4.

	TITLE	INT. RATE	MO. PAYMENT	BALANCE	ORIGINAL # OF PMTS REMAINING	(Approximate) REVISED # OF PMTS REMAINING
1	Orthodontist	0.0%	$ 62.50	$ 500.00	8.00	1.03
2	Medical Doctor	0.0%	$ 25.00	$ 475.00	19.00	1.88
3	Credit Card B	21.0%	$ 74.22	$ 1,243.42	20.00	3.90
4	Credit Card C	16.5%	$ 75.50	$ 2,480.00	44.00	7.51
5	Credit Card A	19.9%	$ 25.02	$ 899.93	55.18	8.72
6	Home Equity Loan	9.9%	$ 77.00	$ 3,625.98	59.86	13.01
7	Auto Payment	7.9%	$ 202.00	$ 9,981.16	59.97	21.70
8	Mortgage	6.5%	$ 890.53	$ 137,440.00	334.65	113.55
9		0.0%	$ -	$ -		-
10		0.0%	$ -	$ -		-
11		0.0%	$ -	$ -		-
12		0.0%	$ -	$ -		-
13		0.0%	$ -	$ -		-
14		0.0%	$ -	$ -		-
15		0.0%	$ -	$ -		-
16		0.0%	$ -	$ -		-
17		0.0%	$ -	$ -		-
18		0.0%	$ -	$ -		-
19		0.0%	$ -	$ -		-
20		0.0%	$ -	$ -		-
	TOTAL NUMBER OF PAYMENTS: (Months)				113.55	113.55
	DIVIDED BY 12 = (Years)					9.46

DEBT ELIMINATION WORKSHEET

STEP 1 - IDENTIFICATION OF DEBTS

List all debts, including your mortgage, credit cards, automobile, second mortgage, etc. Input information only in the green shaded cells.

TITLE	INT. RATE	MO. PAYMENT	BALANCE	Approximate # OF PMTS REMAINING	Approximate LEVEL OF REAL DEBT
			TOTAL AMOUNT BORROWED $		$

STEP 2 - HOW FAR ARE YOU REALLY IN DEBT?

$

This number is calculated by multiplying each monthly payment by the remaining number of payments for that debt, then adding all of the resulting amounts as shown above.

STEP 3 - HOW LONG FOR PAYOFF?

POWER PMT. =

Don't forget to put in your power payment as discussed in Chapter 4.

The debts are listed in order of original payoff; the one that would naturally be paid off first is listed first and so on. Don't forget to enter your power payment as discussed in Chapter 4.

TITLE	INT. RATE	MO. PAYMENT	BALANCE	ORIGINAL # OF PMTS REMAINING	(Approximate) REVISED # OF PMTS REMAINING
1		$	$		
2		$	$		
3		$	$		
4		$	$		
5		$	$		
6		$	$		
7		$	$		
8		$	$		
9		$	$		
10		$	$		
11		$	$		
12		$	$		
13		$	$		
14		$	$		
15		$	$		
16		$	$		
17		$	$		
18		$	$		
19		$	$		
20		$	$		

TOTAL NUMBER OF PAYMENTS: _____ (Months)

DIVIDED BY 12 = _____ (Years)

POWER PAYMENT PLAN

INSTRUCTIONS:

Step 1: By careful budgeting, set aside 10 to 15 percent of your take-home pay.

Step 2: Apply the 10 to 15 percent toward the payment of debt 1. Make out a check for this amount. Write on the check, "FOR PRINCIPAL ONLY" and apply it to debt 1. Write a second check for the regular monthly payment. Continue to make the regular monthly payment and the power payment for the remainder of your debts.

Step 3: When debt 1 is paid in full, make out a check for the 10 to 15 percent of your take-home pay the minimum monthly payment of debt 1. Apply this check toward the principal of debt 2. Make out a check for the regular monthly amount as well. Continue this procedure for each debt until all are paid in full.

Note: if you have more than 8 debts, simply make an additional copy of this template and place half of your debts on each.

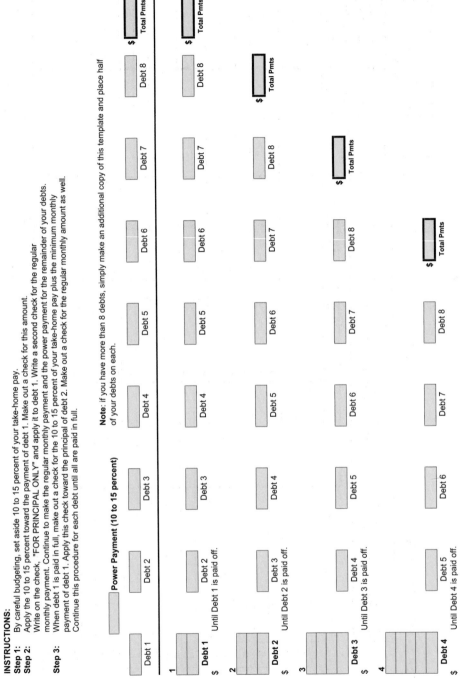

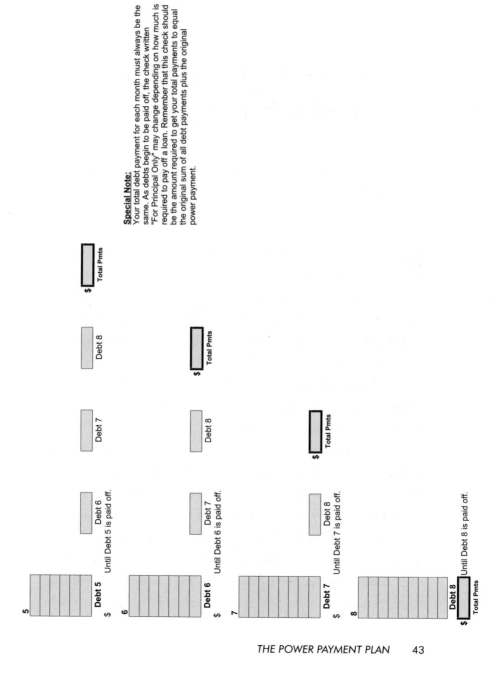

Special Note:
Your total debt payment for each month must always be the same. As debts begin to be paid off, the check written "For Principal Only" may change depending on how much is required to pay off a loan. Remember that this check should be the amount required to get your total payments to equal the original sum of all debt payments plus the original power payment.

CHAPTER 5

Other Methods of Debt Elimination

Pay the debt thou hast contracted. . . . Release thyself from bondage.

—D&C 19:35

For most families, the Power Payment Plan explained in the previous chapter is the safest and most efficient way to repay debts. This is a tried and true system that goes by many different names. It is not an original concept. Most credit counselors use some form of this system to help their clients eliminate their debts, and they charge them somewhere in the neighborhood of 5 percent of their debt load each month just to manage the power payment formula. Most people do not need to pay someone else to do what they can do for themselves.

There are great rewards to managing your own debt, repaying it on your own terms, and working at your own pace. First, you will dispatch your debt more quickly. Why? Because the total amount saved from your monthly budget will be expended toward the elimination of your debt through the power payment. In other words, you will owe no other institution a fee that would be subtracted from your power payment. In this manner, you will save both years and money. Second, by applying the system of debt repayment for yourself, you discipline and refine your personal spending habits.

Most important, you will be working as a team—husband, wife, and perhaps even your children—toward a common goal. There is no way to calculate the benefit this will be to your family. Squabbles over finance are the single most frequent cause of marital instability. But those squabbles disappear when all parties are working on the same page, with the same values, toward the same ultimate goal. These rewards form a bond that we call self-reliance. That independent, hard-working spirit will permeate every other aspect of your life. That's what all the prophets have been teaching us since the restoration of the gospel in these latter-days. Self-reliance is a preeminent tenet of our religion.

Before we leave our discussion of debt, we would be remiss if we didn't provide you with other options of debt elimination. Let's explore a few of these options.

Sell, Trade, or Cash In an Asset

Let's start with the easiest alternative and work toward some of the harder ones. One of the easiest ways to eliminate at least some of your debt is to sell something and use the cash to pay off another debt. Look carefully at your assets. Could you sell something you own to pay off any of your debts? Do you own cars, property, stocks, insurance policies, or other assets? Could you liquidate savings accounts? Do you own jewelry, heirlooms, or any other property assets that could be traded for the principal of one or more of your debts?

Some debts can be exchanged by selling and replacing your property with something less expensive. Can you get by with a less expensive car or home? Even if you decide that the Power Payment process looks good to you, it may be well to consider if you are perhaps living above your means. In chapter **8** we'll provide you with a worksheet that lists your assets and the total amount of your debt on a single page. Such a comparison allows you to see at a glance where additional money is or how eliminating a debt will significantly improve your financial picture.

Buying, selling, or trading assets for debts may sound like obvious solutions; but sometimes we get so close to our problems that we ignore even the obvious. We all know of families, strapped for cash, that forget they have money in savings accounts, bonds, or stocks that can be either sold or withdrawn. Some remember but are stubbornly reluctant to use it. Maybe that is because they determined long ago never to touch that money. Perhaps the thought of selling seems taboo. But isn't it worth spending these resources to buy a little peace of mind? You, ultimately, are the best judge. These are decisions that must be considered as a family unit. It would not be fair to unilaterally decide to sell, trade, or cash in an asset without all parties feeling comfortable with the decision.

Balance Transfers

Most credit cards offer a service known as the balance transfer. This is how it works. The balance owed on another card can be transferred to a new account or to an existing account with a lower rate. Many Americans have taken advantage of this service as a way to dismiss some of their debts.

Doug and Diane were just such a couple. They felt they had discovered a unique and simple way to manage their debt. Credit card offers plugged their mailbox every day. Some of the offers were for astonishingly low interest rates and many offered the option of transferring their balance for a new, lower rate. For years, Doug and Diane threw these offers in the trash, and then one particularly depressing day as they struggled to pay their bills, they opened one of those offers. It looked tempting.

"Aha!" Doug thought to himself, "If I transfer the balance of a higher interest credit card to this new one, I will save money. In addition, if I transfer now, I have an additional month to make payments. This will give me more money next month to spend toward other bills. What a great idea!"

It sounded so exciting that he fairly giggled as he filled out the application. Sure enough, once the application was approved, he was easily able to transfer the balance of his biggest card to the new one. But the pressure of his finances did not ease and he sought to widen this remedy. With a big enough line of credit, he could do the same thing for all his credit card debts.

It worked well for a while, but eventually, as is almost always the case, the new cards raised their interest rates. Most of those ridiculously low rates are only introductory offers. "No problem," thought Doug, "New offers are pouring in every day. I'll just keep transferring balances and move them again before the rates rises again." There was no end to the credit card applications, and he could constantly transfer the balances before the introductory offers expired and the higher interest rates kicked in.

Doug and Diane loved this new system. By constantly trans-ferring balances, there were often grace periods where some debts didn't have to be paid. This freed up money from month to month, buying much-needed time and providing extra cash for additional purchases. With a little extra cash and a whole new line of credit, it became way too tempting to add to the credit card debt. Doug and Diane looked forward to each new credit card offer, always searching for the best deals.

This went on for quite a while, but the day of reckoning arrived as it always does. Diane found herself at the mall undergoing an embarrassing and humiliating experience. As she handed her first card to the clerk, she was embarrassed to have the young clerk inform her that her credit had been refused.

"No problem," she thought, "I'll try another one."

Well, Diane pulled out three more cards and each one was refused. They had all been simply "maxed out."

Doug and Diane's options at this point had narrowed significantly. They tried to get a loan to pay off all the credit card debts, only to find that with so many cards and so many balances bouncing back and forth they had become a poor credit risk. No one would grant them a loan. Doug and Diane learned that transferring balances to avoid making monthly payments carries with it a high price.

Doug and Diane's situation is deliberately exaggerated to teach a not-so-exaggerated lesson. Transferring balances may seem like a solution to a monthly cash flow problem, but the risks involved are steep. Credit card customers can be lulled into a false sense of security. Too many have discovered that even if they make prompt payments, and even if they do not "max-out" their lines of credit, at some point life will provide them an economic hurdle and they will stand atop a scary precipice. With credit cards, even one missed or late payment can mean a high-risk interest rate—not just with that one card but on every other card you own. That is because credit card companies keep track of one another.

Just how bad can it get? Well, recently some credit card companies raised their rates to a whopping 29.9 percent annual percentage rate (APR) for their high-risk customers.

How does this translates into actual cash? If you owe just $1,000 and can afford only minimum monthly payments of about 3 percent the total, it would take you twenty-four years to pay back that $1,000, and you would have spent $3,655.73 in interest alone.

This assumes you incur no additional debt. If that's not bad enough, consider what happens when that debt is $3,000! How does $13,459 in interest spread over forty-two years sound to you? (see "Card Rates Skyrocket," *Deseret News,* February 10, 2002, M1).

There is an additional trap inherent with a credit card that must be mentioned before ending our discussion of balance transfers. When interest rates are falling, consumers generally shop around for a smaller monthly, minimum payment. But if that shopping occurs too frequently, it makes you look to a potential creditor like a person eager to take on new debt. It can even affect your credit rating. Every time you make an application for a new credit card, your lender requests a credit report. A person who jumps from credit card to credit card is not considered a good investment. What this means is that when it comes time to make a major purchase, such as a home or a car, your credit rating will say that you are not a good risk. You could find yourself being turned down even though you never fell behind on your monthly payments.

Debt Consolidation Loans

Debt consolidation loans are the most highly advertised and most attractive methods of debt elimination in today's market. For some people they have become the ideal method of paying off debt while preserving enough income to meet necessary expenses. Despite their popularity, there are traps involved with debt consolidation loans that you need to be aware of before entering into a binding agreement.

A debt consolidation loan is a loan that combines all of your smaller debts into a larger loan, usually with a lower interest rate and a lower monthly payment. It sounds like a great idea, but to make it work requires a great deal of self-control and discipline.

Problems arise when some people discover that the lower

monthly payment of the consolidated loan has freed up enough income to allow them a "splurge" or two. One "splurge" almost always leads to two and then three, and, before they know it, they not only have a consolidation loan to pay, but lots of new small debts as well. They are in worse shape than they were before.

Karen found out the hard way that a debt consolidation loan seems attractive but does not solve her deep-seated problem. Karen took out a debt consolidation loan just three years ago. She consolidated $42,000 in debt into one loan with a much lower interest rate and a considerably lower monthly payment. She felt relieved the day her loan closed and she walked away from the bank. She thought she had conquered her problem.

But, unfortunately for Karen, that was not where it ended. She still couldn't control her spending. In three short years she massed a new $59,000 debt outside her consolidation loan. That left her with the original $42,000 to repay and an additional $59,000. Instead of being $42,000 in debt, she was $101,000 in debt.

Not everyone who takes out a debt consolidation loan finds themselves in Karen's shoes, but many do. Getting out of debt involves changes in habits and in lifestyle. There are no quick fixes. If you are looking at a debt consolidation loan as a quick and painless solution for your financial woes, then you will likely be disappointed and could soon find yourself in a worse situation than you are presently in.

In addition, if a debt consolidation loan seems like a good solution to you, be prepared to do a little research and a whole lot of shopping around. You will find that terms and conditions vary from institution to institution. Some debt consolidation loans have excellent terms and sound, financial backing while others are traps somewhat akin to loan sharking. Know what you are tackling before you get into it. Consolidation cannot make your debts disappear—you will still pay them and it may well be that the longer term of the loan means that in the end you will pay far more than if you had paid by the original terms and with the original interest. Inform yourself and calculate costs before you make a commitment.

Home Equity Loans

Like the debt consolidation loan, you can consolidate all your revolving credit secured by the equity in your home. In fact, some debt consolidation loans are home equity loans. Because home mortgages carry lower interest rates, a home equity loan becomes an attractive option. The problem with using your equity as collateral on your loan is that it jeopardizes the roof over your head. This is never a good idea.

A home equity loan works exactly like the debt consolidation loan. It is not a painless, magical pill but a solution that requires a great deal of self-control to make it work. And there is one additional caution: Some home equity loans, which operate with a line of credit, place an additional and sometimes hidden jeopardy to your home. Some institutions place an immediate lien against your property not just for the amount you borrow but for the entire line of credit they offer you.

Let's show you what we mean. The Smiths needed to borrow $20,000 to get rid of a few nagging bills and make some remodels on their home at the same time. They were extended a line of credit for $50,000 but prudently, they thought, borrowed only the $20,000 they figured they'd need. Eventually the Smiths paid the $20,000 in full. A year went by. The bank with which they'd taken out their home equity loan sent them a bill for their line of credit fee. The Smiths were shocked. They'd paid that loan off a year ago. They called the bank thinking there was a mistake. "No," they were told, "they owed a fee for the $50,000 line of credit." Then to their horror they discovered something even worse. The bank had placed a lien on their home for $50,000, the entire line of credit. It mattered not that they did not use that line of credit, the lien was still there. The Smiths had to go through the painful process of removing the lien. But the Smiths were lucky. Had they discovered this when they were in the process of selling their house, that $50,000 lien would have been far worse.

It is important to point out that not all lending institutions create such monstrous terms on home equity loans, but the buyer should beware. There are terms on every loan, and it pays to acquaint yourself with each and every one of them. Loans may seem quick and painless, but they always carry risks. Investigate before you sign on the dotted line.

Let's talk about an additional risk that you may not even consider when consolidating debts that use the equity in your home as collateral. What if the housing market dips after you have taken out your loan? If you should need to sell your home in that situation, you may be faced with a huge loss. Randy and Linda had taken out a loan for $20,000 against the equity in their home. Time passed. Randy and Linda needed to sell their home, but the housing market had taken a dip. Now their home was worth $20,000 less. But the loan was still there. To recoup the money was impossible and they were faced with a $20,000 loss.

Summary

At this point let's do a little summary. Balance transfers, debt consolidation loans, and home equity loans require self-control and discipline to work. Making voluntary power payments is, therefore, far and away the better option. Why? Because it requires the same kind of self-control and discipline but carries with it none of the inherent risks. The added advantage is that this method of repayment makes you dependent on no one but yourself. That is a clear advantage.

Options to Those with Greater Need

Up to this point we have discussed methods of debt elimination for people who have not yet missed payments or gotten themselves into serious financial hot water. But what if you are in more serious trouble? What if the creditors have come calling and your options are running out?

The last two methods of debt elimination—credit counseling and bankruptcy—are for those people who have debts far beyond their control. They are last-attempt methods and should be taken only when you feel that there is no other way. They are good methods and they are legal; but only those who find no other way out should take them. They carry with them some additional stigmas that could affect you and your family for many years to come.

Steve Rhode, who co-founded Myvesta.org, a credit counseling service, says: "Bankruptcy is a financial solution for an emotional problem." And, he adds, "debt is never about money" (in Paul J. Lim, "Digging Your Way Out of Debt," *US News & World Report,* March 19, 2001, 59). For some people there is no other way out than these last two methods of debt elimination. For them finances are part of a much larger problem.

Credit Counseling

Whether they are called Consumer Credit Counseling, Debtor's Anonymous, or the National Foundation for Credit Counseling, there are many agencies that deal with counseling debtors and helping them back on the road to recovery. Some professional debt-relief organizations help the debtor to recover but do not focus on *how* he got himself into debt; while other services spend a great deal of time exploring the *how* and seeking solutions to an emotional problem.

Because there are far too many organizations to adequately cover, we will not attempt to explore or recommend any specific programs. Most of these services operate on the same principles and do a capable job of helping people out of some desperate situations. But not all organizations that claim to help the debtor are reliable, licensed, and have the integrity to do so. Many of the more reliable services are associated with what is known as the Association of Independent Consumer Credit Counseling Agencies (AICCCA). We are grateful for their website, which has provided us with some guidelines to assist you in a search for reliable credit counseling.

Here is a list of what you should look for before you sign on with a credit counseling service; the guidelines were gleaned from a quick review on the Internet:

- They must be a non-profit 501(c)(3) organization.
- They should be licensed to operate in the state in which you reside.
- They should maintain a satisfactory rating with the Better Business Bureau.
- They must begin resolution of client complaints within 10 days of notification.
- They must have an independent board of directors, the majority of which cannot be compensated employees of the agency or related by blood or marriage to other board members or employees.
- They must have operated continuously in the state in which they are organized for at least one year.

- They must maintain a permanent physical business location and not operate solely out of a post office box.
- They must meet all state licensing, registration, bonding, and statutory requirements.
- They must be open during normal business hours.
- They must provide counseling to anyone who desires it.
- They must employ only counselors certified by an AICCCA-accepted body within one year of completing their six month "in agency" training program.
- Compensation for counselors cannot be based on the outcome of the counseling process.
- Service is provided to the public regardless of ability to pay.
- Fees will not exceed a maximum set-up fee of $75 or exceed $50 per month for maintenance of an account. Other fees for additional services must be reasonable.
- No fee can be charged for credit repair.
- All deposits made by clients should be dispatched to creditors in a timely manner.
- Consult www.aiccca.org for more details.

Independent credit counselors work in a similar manner. The client pays a monthly fee or deposit. From that deposit the credit counselor pays the client's creditors at lower monthly payments and reduced interest charges. Late fees are waived. Counselors are available twenty-four hours a day, seven days a week. All counselors are licensed and certified by the state in which you reside.

The drawback of most credit counseling services is that they will only work for you after you have exhausted most other avenues of debt elimination. Those who are in over their heads but have not yet missed a payment may not be eligible for this recourse. Some counseling services will not take clients until they can no longer meet minimum payments.

There is another caution to this method that bears discussing. Though client's accounts are confidential, the very fact that credit counselors contact creditors casts a pall over your reputation. This is not a step to be taken hastily or lightly. Think this through before you act. On the other hand, if this is something you truly need to handle your problem, then do not hesitate to take this step. Always remember, having a debt problem does not make you a bad person; you risk your reputation only if you do not act and act soon enough.

Bankruptcy

This form of debt elimination is the ultimate in "last resort" methods. It is the atomic bomb of debt elimination because it carries with it such lasting repercussions. It is legal and it is often necessary. Many families have been forced to take this step through no real fault of their own; others have found it to be a convenient way of dodging their debts. But beware. There is good reason why so many experts have labeled bankruptcy as the "ten-year mistake."

There are, for the most part, two kinds of bankruptcy protection available to the consumer: Chapter 7 and Chapter 13. A Chapter 7 bankruptcy absolves you of all your debts except back child support, student loans, taxes, or withdrawals in excess of $1,000 made within twenty days of the declared bankruptcy. Your goods will be taken and sold at auction to pay your creditors. You are allowed to keep only some of the equity in your home and in your car, some household goods, and any trade tools you may possess. This form of bankruptcy carries a stain on your credit report for ten years and you are not allowed to file again for another six years.

A Chapter 13 bankruptcy allows you to keep all of your assets, but the court orders a plan for you to pay a certain portion of your debt over a period of time and the creditors are expected to take what you are ordered to pay as payment in full. The court determines the amount based upon your ability to pay. The period of time is anywhere from three to five years.

A word to the wise: Although bankruptcy stains your credit record for only ten years, forever after whenever you apply for a loan or a job, you may be asked if you *ever* filed for bankruptcy and you will be forced to disclose it again. This can happen for the rest of your life. In addition, though bankruptcy protection is not a matter of public record, those who have filed may be required to pay their loss through their wages. This makes your employer aware of your situation. An employer, even though aware, cannot legally discriminate against you because of bankruptcy, but you must know that it could be potentially embarrassing.

In addition, do not let anyone tell you that you must file for bankruptcy protection because your debts exceed a certain amount. Find an expert, someone you can trust whom you know to be a person of integrity and good sense and ask them honestly to counsel your special situation. Bankruptcy is your legal right and is provided for your protection; but it is not a step to be taken lightly.

Also, be aware that the following debts are not erased with bankruptcy:

- taxes
- spousal and child support
- debts arising out of willful or malicious conduct
- liability from driving under the influence of alcohol
- debts from any prior bankruptcy
- most student loans
- criminal fines and penalties
- attorney's fees

If you are one of those unfortunate few who have found themselves in this kind of financial distress, you need to remember that you are not alone and that your financial problems do not make you a terrible person. There are many good, well-intentioned, and compassionate people who have found themselves in this extreme distress. Bankruptcy does not in and of itself jeopardize your standing in the Church. Restoring your self-confidence after a bankruptcy is paramount in importance. For that reason alone, read on. Sensible spending will restore your feelings of self-worth and you will learn whatever is necessary to make yourself self-reliant one day in the near future.

CHAPTER 6

Debt-Free: A Philosophy

If there is any one thing that will bring peace and contentment into the human heart, and into the family, it is to live within our means.

—PRESIDENT HEBER J. GRANT

We have begun our instruction on becoming debt-free with five chapters on basic debt elimination. We've made a case against debt and given you some options on just how you might eliminate it from your life. We could end here. We realize, however, that what we have provided thus far is simply not enough. How do you find money to make a power payment from an already stretched budget? How do you keep up with the demand of your growing family and their expanding needs? How do you pay for the constant bombardment of crises that life hands you on an almost daily basis without going right back into debt? It isn't easy.

It goes without saying that one of our primary goals is to be completely self-reliant. Self-reliance is basic to the doctrine and practice of our religion. From the beginning of time, mortals have been counseled by God and his prophets to be self-reliant, to earn their own way, to be independent, and to avoid temporal or spiritual bondage. Why does God expect his children to become self-reliant? Elder Alexander B. Morrison in his book *Visions of Zion* has provided us with the answer. "Self-reliance is closely tied to freedom. . . . We cannot be free if we are not self-reliant. Put another way, self-reliance is a prerequisite for freedom, and dependence is the enemy of freedom. . . . Independence and self-reliance thus are critical keys to spiritual growth. Whenever we are in a situation that threatens self-reliance, we will find that freedom is threatened too" (Salt Lake City: Deseret Book, 1993, 111).

In the early days of the restored gospel of Christ, the counsel was the same. Brigham Young taught the Saints of his own day the importance of this principle:

> We want you henceforth to be a self-sustaining people. Hear it, O Israel! hear it, neighbors, friends, and enemies, this is what the Lord requires of this people.
>
> Ye Latter-day Saints, learn to sustain yourselves . . . if you cannot obtain all you wish for today, learn to do without that which you cannot purchase and pay for; and bring your minds into subjection that you must and will live within your means.
>
> Who are deserving of praise? The persons who take care of themselves or the ones who always trust in the great mercies of the Lord to take care of them? It is just as consistent to expect that the Lord will supply us with fruit when we do not plant the trees; or that when we do not plow and sow and are saved the labor of harvesting, we should cry to the Lord to save us from want, as to ask him to save us from the consequences of our own, folly, disobedience and waste. . . .
>
> Brethren, learn. You have learned a good deal, it is true; but learn more; learn to sustain yourselves . . . save . . . against a day of scarcity. . . .
>
> Instead of searching after what the Lord is going to do for us, let us inquire what we can do for ourselves. (In John A. Widtsoe, comp., *Discourses of Brigham Young* [Salt Lake City: Deseret Book, 1954], 293.)

To really achieve that self-reliance we have to learn how to manage our day-to-day spending, provide for our future, and pay for our emergencies. This requires careful planning. Planning may not solve all those unforeseen financial woes that are sure to come your way, but it certainly can minimize their effects. No matter what your income or how financially secure you think you are, you must have a plan for spending your money. Fighting, worrying, even panicking over money will only cause instability and will not contribute to the peace and security of family life.

President Gordon B. Hinckley has counseled: "I am satisfied that money is the root of more trouble in marriage than all other causes combined. . . . There would be fewer rash decisions, fewer unwise investments, fewer consequent losses, fewer bankruptcies if husbands and wives would counsel together on such matters and unitedly seek counsel from others" (*Cornerstones of a Happy Home*, pamphlet [Salt Lake City: Intellectual Reserve, Inc., 1984], 8, 9).

Many people are embarrassed to admit that they need help with how to spend their money more sensibly. You are not alone. We are all in much the same boat. We've all spent foolishly at some time or another. We've all regretted some financial decisions we've made. But we can all improve. No matter what stage of life you now find yourself in, it is never too late to back up and begin again. Your dreams are almost within reach.

So let's begin at the beginning. Let's discover where you are. Take this little assessment quiz and be on your way to being truly debt free. If you are married, fulfill this little assignment together. The quiz is designed to help you assess your goals and jointly solidify them, to allow you to discover your weaknesses, and to provide a foundation of consensus on basic money management issues. In the next few chapters we will help you learn to plan your spending more efficiently so that you might truly be debt-free. In other words, we hope you will soon be able to manage your money before it manages you.

Pre-Assessment Quiz

Circle *yes* if you agree with the statement, *no* if you disagree with the statement, or *N/A* if it does not apply to your situation. Be as honest as possible.

Philosophy

Yes No N/A   1. Becoming wealthy is not one of our top priorities. There are more important things than making a living.

Yes No N/A   2. We find it easy to handle money but are eager to find better ways to manage it.

Yes No N/A   3. We do not engage in ruthless business dealings. We do not think such practices are smart business.

Yes No N/A   4. When money is tight, we still donate to worthy causes.

Yes No N/A   5. We enjoy our vocations. To us they are more than just a way to make a good living.

Principles and General Rules

Yes No N/A   6. We are able to make our income exceed our expenses.

Yes No N/A   7. We live within our means.

Yes No N/A   8. We are good at planning our spending.

Yes No N/A   9. We use a budget.

Yes No N/A   10. We have a detailed record-keeping system.

Yes No N/A   11. We are honest in all our financial dealings.

Yes No N/A   12. We have a scheduled time to review budgets and expenses each week.

Yes No N/A   13. We are out of debt.

Yes No N/A   14. We discuss and know the difference between our wants and our needs.

Yes No N/A   15. As a couple we work together on our financial plans.

Planning

Yes No N/A   16. At the end of the month, we always have money left over.

Yes No N/A   17. We buy only that which we have planned to buy, even if there's something we want on sale.

Yes No N/A   18. We have credit cards but we pay them in full each month.

Yes No N/A   19. We know where every penny went and can give an accurate account of all our expenditures.

Yes No N/A   20. We avoid carrying much cash.

Yes No N/A   21. We set aside funds for anticipated future purchases.

Yes No N/A   22. We always have the money on hand to pay cash for items.

Yes No N/A   23. We understand how interest works and make it work for us.

Yes No N/A   24. We never live on next week's check.

Yes No N/A   25. We have both an accessible and a long-term savings program.

Yes No N/A   26. We have a "rainy day" fund for emergencies.

Yes No N/A   27. We have adequate health and life insurance coverage for our family.

Yes No N/A   28. Our home/apartment is insured against disasters.

Yes No N/A   29. We avoid risky investments that could jeopardize our living expenses.

Yes No N/A   30. We have a family organization to provide financial support in time of crisis.

Inventory

Yes No N/A   31. We know what our income is.

Yes No N/A   32. We know our total cash assets.

Yes No N/A   33. We know our total financial worth.

Yes No N/A 34. We know when insurance and taxes come due and are prepared with funds on hand. We have put aside funds for high expense periods such as Christmas, back-to-school clothing, and vacations.

Yes No N/A 35. We use times of peak income to balance peak expense periods. We save our bonuses and extra checks to balance for those months when our expenses will be greater.

Goals

Yes No N/A 36. We have prioritized our financial needs in writing.

Yes No N/A 37. We do not allow our hobbies to jeopardize money used for our basic needs.

Yes No N/A 38. We know what our lifetime financial goals are.

Yes No N/A 39. We know what our year's financial goals are.

Yes No N/A 40. We know what our next month's financial goals are.

Debt Management

Yes No N/A 41. We are good at avoiding debt.

Yes No N/A 42. We have a listing of all our debts and know when they will be paid off.

Yes No N/A 43. We understand exactly how much interest we will pay on our debts.

Yes No N/A 44. We are working to get out of debt as fast as possible.

Yes No N/A 45. We are serious about reducing our debt.

Savings

Yes No N/A 46. We save at least 10 percent of our take-home pay.

Yes No N/A 47. We have a savings account for large upcoming purchases.

Yes No N/A 48. We are saving for our retirement.

Yes No N/A 49. We do not withdraw from our savings unless it is an emergency or a planned purchase.

Yes No N/A 50. We understand the wisdom of "a penny saved is a penny earned."

Cutting Costs

Yes No N/A   51. We work as hard at spending our money as we do earning it.

Yes No N/A   52. We have analyzed where we spend money and have found ways to reduce expenses.

Yes No N/A   53. We set aside "mad money." This allows us some freedom to spend without accountability.

Yes No N/A   54. We go to the library or request publications to study ways to cut expenses.

Yes No N/A   55. We feel that our lifestyle and standard of living fit well within our income.

Yearly Strategy

Yes No N/A   56. We keep a yearly history of actual expenses for which future budgets can be based.

Yes No N/A   57. We are aware of seasonal best buys and plan yearly for them.

Yes No N/A   58. We like to look at the whole picture of a year's expenses so that we can be flexible in planning.

Yes No N/A   59. We keep yearly records of expenses for at least three years in case of a tax audit.

Yes No N/A   60. Debt elimination is part of our yearly strategy.

Monthly Strategy

Yes No N/A   61. We think of budgets as a positive plan for financial success rather than a hardship.

Yes No N/A   62. We are willing to make the time commitment necessary to plan financial strategies.

Yes No N/A   63. We adhere to a detailed budget, instead of just balancing our checkbook.

Yes No N/A   64. We avoid stress by making it a practice to never argue about how money was used or to assess blame when it comes time to figure finances.

Yes No N/A   65. We realize that expenses and budgets must change
with each season of our life. Transitions from
being single to married, to raising a growing family,
and to retirement are all accounted for and we
can adjust to the financial challenges each aspect
of life brings.

Scoring the Quiz

If you have taken this quiz, you have already passed it with flying
colors. You are a winner. Use the concepts presented to begin a discussion and build a consensus of your family's philosophy toward spending.
This exercise was not meant to frighten or embarrass you. There is not
an individual or a couple on this planet who would not benefit from taking an opportunity now and again to assess where they are and how efficient they are at managing their money.

CHAPTER 7

Debt-Free Planning

*Wherefore, do not spend money for that which is of no
worth, nor your labor for that which cannot satisfy. . . .
Feast upon that which perisheth not, . . . and let your soul
delight in fatness.*

—2 NEPHI 9:51

W here does managing your money fit on your list of priorities? Does being debt-free really matter to you? How does
your desire for wealth work together with your values and goals in
life? What would you do with more money if you had it? What
changes would you expect in your character and the way you live
if you had enough money and you no longer had to worry about
funds? To what ends would you go to obtain wealth?

Three Keys to Financial Success

The answers to these questions determine your philosophy
of spending money. To begin to control your day-to-day spending habits without marital discord, it is best to start by develop-
ing a plan you can both agree upon. Here are three sound
suggestions:

1. Be honest in all your financial dealings. Honesty solves
problems; it never creates them. We need to pay our bills

promptly and completely. Honesty establishes a foundation of trust in all our relationships. It allows us a clean reputation and a good credit history.

2. Schedule time for and keep an accurate record of finances, including income, expenses, and a budget. You must know how you spent your money before you can assess where to make changes. In addition, you'll only be guessing your true financial picture if you don't have a system for tracking your purchases and for paying your bills. A good record-keeping system is worth its weight in gold. There is no possible way for you to get ahead unless you have something to analyze and assess, to know how and where to save money and pay off your debt.

Obviously an initial meeting will take some time. You will have to spend some time gathering records and old bills before you meet. You might consider scheduling an entire family home evening to begin your planning process. Once certain specific decisions have been made and a plan put into place, you will find that the amount of time it takes to manage your finances will decrease significantly. Most experts will tell you that it will take at least three months before you really develop a feel for your budget, and then your efforts will become second nature.

From that time forward you can establish a set time each week to record and analyze income and expenses. These sessions will take only a minimum amount of time which will lessen with each passing month as your planning methods improve. Some families find Saturday morning convenient because they know they spend more money on Saturday than any other day of the week. Whatever day you choose, make the time and place consistent. That way, the time you spend is cut to a minimum. It should never take more than half an hour to work on your finances if you are committed.

Planning how to spend your money is the key to financial management. Some families' ideas of financial management is just to record their purchases. Obviously, that is not enough. You'll never get a grip on your dollar—never get ahead financially—if all you do is record your purchases and hope somehow that there will be money to cover it all at the end of every month. You must plan before you spend. You must utilize the time with your family to make a detailed plan. You must listen to everyone's needs and you must assess and assign specific amounts to each category of your financial plan. Only then can you go back and look at your actual expenditures and make any reasonable assessment of your success.

Think of your home as a business. A successful business would not think of trying to function without a plan, and neither should a home. Many people without a spending plan think they are maintaining their finances adequately until they suddenly find themselves caught in a monetary fiscal crisis. At that point it will probably require more than financial Band-Aids; it will probably require financial surgery. With a plan, you can anticipate surprises and avoid catastrophe.

Involve children in planning your spending so they can learn how to spend more sensibly. Talk about plans for spending and ask their opinions. In the future, your children will become better-prepared adults. They will be more realistic and responsible in planning their own monetary goals.

Think of your planning time as a game. Make it fun and exciting. Correct planning can provide hundreds of additional dollars for every hour you spend. Today's society is far too complex to allow you to exist without a plan.

3. Learn to distinguish between wants and needs and then prioritize your spending accordingly. When wants replace needs, the family budget soon runs into deep trouble. Advertisements stimulate consumer appetites. Luxuries and convenience all too often displace genuine need. Many young married people try to get too many of their wants too soon. Overindulgence leads to an overabundance of consumer debt, which jeopardizes future earnings and financial stability.

Careful analysis of needs and wants is an important step in wise personal money management. You might think that you and your spouse always agree on which expenditures in your monthly spending plan pay for needs and which pay for wants. But each individual perceives things from a different perspective. You have to know what your spouse thinks are needs and you must listen and understand. You have to know what your children think are needs and you must listen and understand. This is an essential discussion. If your spouse has a need that you consider only a frivolous expense, then it's time to reassess. Mutual understanding and compromise can overcome almost every disagreement.

What Are Needs and What Are Wants?

Needs are essential expenses. Needs include housing, electricity, heat, food, and medical expenses. Additional family needs might include fuel and service to your automobile, tithes and offerings, clothing, and household maintenance. Many of our vocations carry with them specific needs. Farmers need basic farm equipment and they must keep that equipment in good, working order. Businesses need computers. Musicians need musical instruments. Salespeople need reliable automobiles if they are required to travel to and from their clientele. Needs are basic and generally easy to determine, but sometimes the line between needs and wants becomes clouded.

Sherri was anxious to replace the air-conditioning system in her home. The old system was unreliable and created for her a miserable working environment. Her husband, Bill, felt that a new air-conditioning unit was too costly and beyond the reach of the family budget. To Sherri air-conditioning was a need; to Bill it was only a want. Sherri pointed out that Bill left home every day for an air-conditioned office, while she worked at home suffering from the heat. By the time he returned, the outside temperature had cooled sufficiently so that he did not notice how unbearable the temperature of the house could become.

But at the same time, Sherri also knew that Bill was right about the family budget being stretched. Together they determined that if Sherri could endure just one more miserable summer, they could set aside enough money every month to purchase a new air-conditioning system the following summer. Bill and Sherri learned a basic rule of fulfilling needs and wants and the importance of working together.

Satisfying Both Needs and Wants

Becoming debt-free requires careful planning. We've spent a lot of time, thus far, making this case. As you plan that spending you must really make not one, but three, different plans.

First comes **maintenance planning.** We often refer to this maintenance planning as the family budget. When President Gordon B. Hinckley asks us to "be modest in [our] expenditures" and to "discipline [ourselves] in [our] purchases," we feel that this refers to a maintenance plan, a plan for our day-to-day spending— a family budget ("To the Boys and to the Men," *Ensign*, November 1998, 54).

Budgets are never consistent every month. That is because life is never static, and neither are your spending needs. As economic inflation shrinks your family budget or as your family grows and expands, so do your financial demands.

To be truly debt-free, your family must also make a **future plan.** There are specific and certain costs that come into each of our lives: missions, college education, new cars, weddings, and so on. These certain and known costs are part of what we call the future plan. Future needs can be planned for and achieved. The way is really not as difficult as it sometimes seems. As President Hinckley wisely counseled: "Save a little money regularly, and you will be surprised how it accumulates" ("To Men of the Priesthood," *Ensign,* November 2002, 58).

The third plan is called the **crisis plan.** Into each life come sudden, unexpected expenses. Tragedy and disaster can strike at any moment; no one is immune. Such emergencies are a contributing factor to debt. To be debt-free you have to be in control during emergencies and have money put aside to pay for them so you don't have to run to the bank or expand your lines of credit.

President Hinckley said: "No one knows when emergencies will strike. I am somewhat familiar with the case of a man who was highly successful in his profession. He lived in comfort. He built a large home. Then one day he was suddenly involved in a serious accident. Instantly, without warning, he almost lost his life. He was left a cripple. Destroyed was his earning power. He faced huge medical bills. He had other payments to make. He was helpless before his creditors. One moment he was rich, the next he was broke." ("To the Boys and to the Men," 53).

Whether you are planning for the present, the future, or for a crisis, you can achieve your needs, goals, and even your dreams with a little planning. Before you go on to the next chapter, fill out the Survey of Needs and Wants. Each spouse should fill out the survey separately and then come together to analyze differing responses. Reach a consensus before the initial planning session. Print out the survey from the CD-ROM or use the one that follows.

Survey of Needs and Wants

Husband [ ]   Wife [ ]   Single [ ]

Auto/Transportation

Need	Want	N/A	Subject	Agreement
❑	❑	❑	1. New, used, or second car	❑
❑	❑	❑	2. Repair car	❑
❑	❑	❑	3. Bicycle	❑
❑	❑	❑	4. Boat	❑
❑	❑	❑	5. Motorcycle	❑
❑	❑	❑	6. RV	❑
❑	❑	❑	7. Monthly bus or mass transit pass	❑
❑	❑	❑	8. New tires	❑
❑	❑	❑	9. Fuel	❑
❑	❑	❑	10.	❑

Charity/Contributions

Need	Want	N/A	Subject	Agreement
❑	❑	❑	1. Tithing	❑
❑	❑	❑	2. Church donations	❑
❑	❑	❑	3. United Way	❑
❑	❑	❑	4.	❑
❑	❑	❑	5.	❑

Debt/Credit Cards

Need	Want	N/A	Subject	Agreement
❑	❑	❑	1. Visa/Master card	❑
❑	❑	❑	2. Department store cards	❑
❑	❑	❑	3. American Express card	❑
❑	❑	❑	4.	❑
❑	❑	❑	5.	❑

Education

Need	Want	N/A	Subject	Agreement
❑	❑	❑	1. More education	❑
❑	❑	❑	2. School fees/tuition	❑
❑	❑	❑	3. Books	❑

Need	Want	N/A	Subject	Agreement
❏	❏	❏	4. Lessons (music, art, etc.)	❏
❏	❏	❏	5. Preschool	❏
❏	❏	❏	6. Educational supplies	❏
❏	❏	❏	7. Book clubs	❏
❏	❏	❏	8. Self-improvement course	❏
❏	❏	❏	9. Computer/software	❏
❏	❏	❏	10. Musical instruments	❏
❏	❏	❏	11. Newspaper/magazine subscriptions	❏
❏	❏	❏	12. Internet service	❏
❏	❏	❏	13.	❏
❏	❏	❏	14.	❏
❏	❏	❏	15.	❏

Food

Need	Want	N/A	Subject	Agreement
❏	❏	❏	1. Groceries	❏
❏	❏	❏	2. Eating out once a week	❏
❏	❏	❏	3. Eating junk food and treats daily	❏
❏	❏	❏	4. Having dinner out/special occasions	❏
❏	❏	❏	5. Food supply for one year	❏
❏	❏	❏	6.	❏
❏	❏	❏	7.	❏

Gifts

Need	Want	N/A	Subject	Agreement
❏	❏	❏	1. Anniversary	❏
❏	❏	❏	2. Birthday	❏
❏	❏	❏	3. Wedding or baby showers	❏
❏	❏	❏	4. Christmas	❏
❏	❏	❏	5.	❏

Home/Shelter

Need	Want	N/A	Subject	Agreement
❏	❏	❏	1. New furniture	❏
❏	❏	❏	2. New appliances	❏
❏	❏	❏	3. Gardening or landscaping	❏
❏	❏	❏	4. Housekeeper	❏

Need	Want	N/A		Subject	Agreement
❑	❑	❑	5. Reducing mortgage		❑
❑	❑	❑	6. Home repairs		❑
❑	❑	❑	7. Purchasing new house or remodeling		❑
❑	❑	❑	8. Air conditioning		❑
❑	❑	❑	9. Purchasing new carpet		❑
❑	❑	❑	10. Shop equipment/tools		❑
❑	❑	❑	11. Freezer		❑
❑	❑	❑	12. Video equipment		❑
❑	❑	❑	13. Vacuum cleaner		❑
❑	❑	❑	14. Stereo equipment		❑
❑	❑	❑	15. Interior decorating		❑
❑	❑	❑	16. Painting house		❑
❑	❑	❑	17. Sewing machine/fabric		❑
❑	❑	❑	18.		❑
❑	❑	❑	19.		❑
❑	❑	❑	20.		❑

Insurance

Need	Want	N/A		Subject	Agreement
❑	❑	❑	1. Life insurance		❑
❑	❑	❑	2. Supplemental life insurance		❑
❑	❑	❑	3. Mortgage insurance		❑
❑	❑	❑	4. Health insurance		❑
❑	❑	❑	5. Auto insurance		❑
❑	❑	❑	6. Property insurance		❑
❑	❑	❑	7. Homeowner/rental insurance		❑
❑	❑	❑	8. Travel insurance		❑
❑	❑	❑	9.		❑
❑	❑	❑	10.		❑

Leisure/Recreation

Need	Want	N/A		Subject	Agreement
❑	❑	❑	1. Sports equipment		❑
❑	❑	❑	2. Camping equipment		❑
❑	❑	❑	3. Sporting events tickets		❑

Need	Want	N/A	Subject	Agreement
❏	❏	❏	4. Cultural events tickets	❏
❏	❏	❏	5. Camera equipment	❏
❏	❏	❏	6. Gym membership	❏
❏	❏	❏	7. Toys for kids	❏
❏	❏	❏	8. Cable TV	❏
❏	❏	❏	9. Hobbies	❏
❏	❏	❏	10. Going to movies	❏
❏	❏	❏	11. Mountain cabin	❏
❏	❏	❏	12.	❏
❏	❏	❏	13.	❏
❏	❏	❏	14.	❏

Medical

Need	Want	N/A	Subject	Agreement
❏	❏	❏	1. Dental work/care	❏
❏	❏	❏	2. Doctor visits	❏
❏	❏	❏	3. Hospital visits	❏
❏	❏	❏	4. Prescriptions	❏
❏	❏	❏	5. Glasses/contacts	❏
❏	❏	❏	6. Weight Watchers	❏
❏	❏	❏	7. Marriage counseling	❏
❏	❏	❏	8. Psychiatrist	❏
❏	❏	❏	9.	❏
❏	❏	❏	10.	❏

Personal

Need	Want	N/A	Subject	Agreement
❏	❏	❏	1. Beauty shop/salon trips	❏
❏	❏	❏	2. Haircuts	❏
❏	❏	❏	3. Makeup	❏
❏	❏	❏	4. Toiletries	❏
❏	❏	❏	5.	❏
❏	❏	❏	6.	❏

Other/Miscellaneous

Need	Want	N/A	Subject	Agreement
❏	❏	❏	1. Alimony/child support	❏

			Subject	Agreement
❏	❏	❏	2. Baby-sitter/day care	❏
❏	❏	❏	3. Children's allowance	❏
❏	❏	❏	4. Cleaning supplies	❏
❏	❏	❏	5. Diaper service	❏
❏	❏	❏	6. Mad Money	❏
❏	❏	❏	7. Pet care/veterinarian	❏
❏	❏	❏	8. Postage	❏
❏	❏	❏	9.	❏
❏	❏	❏	10.	❏
❏	❏	❏	11.	❏

Savings/Investments

			Subject	Agreement
❏	❏	❏	1. Missionary fund	❏
❏	❏	❏	2. Real estate	❏
❏	❏	❏	3. Stocks and bonds	❏
❏	❏	❏	4. Rainy day funds	❏
❏	❏	❏	5. Rental properties	❏
❏	❏	❏	6. Money Market accounts	❏
❏	❏	❏	7. Savings account	❏
❏	❏	❏	8. Retirement savings	❏
❏	❏	❏	9. Children's weddings	❏
❏	❏	❏	10.	❏

Taxes

			Subject	Agreement
❏	❏	❏	1. Income taxes	❏
❏	❏	❏	2. Property taxes	❏
❏	❏	❏	3. Auto registration	❏
❏	❏	❏	4. Capital gains tax	❏
❏	❏	❏	5.	❏
❏	❏	❏	6.	❏

Utilities

			Subject	Agreement
❏	❏	❏	1. Cell phone	❏
❏	❏	❏	2. Electricity	❏

Need	Want	N/A	Subject	Agreement
❏	❏	❏	3. Garbage	❏
❏	❏	❏	4. Gas	❏
❏	❏	❏	5. Home heating	❏
❏	❏	❏	6. Sewer	❏
❏	❏	❏	7. Telephone	❏
❏	❏	❏	8. Water	❏
❏	❏	❏	9.	❏
❏	❏	❏	10.	❏

Vacation/Travel

Need	Want	N/A	Subject	Agreement
❏	❏	❏	1. Yearly vacation	❏
❏	❏	❏	2. Weekend getaways	❏
❏	❏	❏	3. Business trips	❏
❏	❏	❏	4. Cruise	❏
❏	❏	❏	5.	❏
❏	❏	❏	6.	❏
❏	❏	❏	7.	❏

Wardrobe/Clothing

Need	Want	N/A	Subject	Agreement
❏	❏	❏	1. New clothing	❏
❏	❏	❏	2. Dry cleaning	❏
❏	❏	❏	3. Laundry service	❏
❏	❏	❏	4. Back-to-school clothes	❏
❏	❏	❏	5. Work clothes	❏
❏	❏	❏	6. Winter clothes	❏
❏	❏	❏	7.	❏
❏	❏	❏	8.	❏

A Maintenance Plan

Learning to live within our means should be a continuing process. We need to work constantly toward keeping ourselves free of financial difficulties.

—MARVIN J. ASHTON

The reason for having a maintenance plan is to support or provide support for yourself and those for whom you are responsible. In this day, it is becoming more and more difficult to provide adequately for our families. What seemed like a high salary a few years ago is no longer adequate. Too many people feel like their pockets are empty and that someone else's hands are constantly reaching in.

Outsmarting Debt

The key to maintenance is to be able to outsmart all those who want to take the money you worked so hard to earn. To stay on sound financial footing requires that you follow certain basic principles: keep your expenses at a lower level than your income, avoid impulse spending, pay as you go, and keep money evaporation at a minimum. Let's show you what we mean.

Expenses Must Be Less than Income

Spending less than you earn will be your key to financial freedom. This will bring financial independence and provide you with control of your own life. Living on less than you earn proves you are smarter than a banker. You learn to beat the banks at their own game. It is not only key to independence and freedom from debt but essential to future planning.

Avoid Impulse Spending

Work as hard at spending your money as you do earning it. Some people look upon shopping as a form of recreation, but recreational shopping can be almost as dangerous as gambling. Don't become a shopaholic. This is a disease of the impulse spender. Learn to know what you are going to buy before you leave the house. Estimate the cost of the items you are going to buy. You may try using the Internet to check prices before going to the stores. Many sites offer comparative pricing, which allows you to get a better idea of quality and price and avoids the impulse to buy just to regret the purchase later. Then when it comes time to make your purchase, stay within the limits you have set. Work at spending your money! Planning is the only way you can spend yourself rich.

Too rigid a budget will probably drive you crazy. Avoid being too rigid. Always keep a slush fund, provide a specific and known amount of money for some amount of impulse buying. Otherwise, what will you do when that once-in-a-lifetime sale comes along and you haven't the funds to take advantage of the savings, or what if you need a break both physically and emotionally and you haven't the funds to cover it? But keep this impulsive buying controlled! A mutually agreed upon amount of money with no accountability can limit your impulses and satisfy your needs. By limiting this amount you'll find both freedom and controlled restraint.

Pay As You Go

You want to get out of debt, right? That's the reason you bought this book. Being debt-free must be instilled within you. You must pay for every expense as it comes and you must pay it in full. What if you haven't got the money, you haven't planned for it, but the occasion comes along when you are tempted to buy? Remember that there is a certain amount of joy that comes when your family plans for and anticipates a purchase. You can often find the money in unexpected places.

The Williams children wanted a new basketball standard. It was beyond the family budget. So Brother Williams made a suggestion to his four children. If they could save enough money from their utility bill over the next few months they could probably afford a new basketball standard. The Williams children went to work. Little elves went behind each person turning off lights and appliances when not in use. The children started limiting their television watching when the bill didn't come down fast enough. Within a few months, the money was raised, the basketball standard was purchased, and, most exciting of all, the family developed new and more efficient habits that stuck with them for a long time thereafter.

Living within your means provides your family with the only sure safety net in an insecure world.

Keep Money "Evaporation" to a Minimum

A problem with money management is the inability to account for money spent. This is especially true of cash. When you carry a large amount of cash it becomes extremely difficult if not impossible to recollect where it was spent and for what it was spent. The money just evaporates.

In addition, carrying cash offers an almost constant temptation to spend for unplanned items. Try to make all your purchases with checks issued for the exact amount and resist the temptation to make them out for a few dollars more. This offers you a record of your expenditures. New systems in some retail outlets, such as discount stores, grocery stores, or gas stations, make it convenient to use a credit card or debit card—another invitation to "evaporation." Keep receipts and deduct them from your budget as soon as is possible.

It doesn't matter how you keep record of your spending, just keep a record. This keeps "evaporation" at a minimum.

Building a Maintenance Plan

Now that you know the principles behind building a maintenance plan, it is time to design your plan. The first step is to use your previous month's spending as a sample. Use the worksheet titled "Last Month's Income and Spending" to help you. To access this worksheet, and all other worksheets in this chapter, go to the main menu and click on Build a maintenance plan. Worksheets are also available at the end of the chapter. The computer will automatically calculate your subtotals and totals for you. If you simply fill out the form with a pencil, make sure you have a calculator nearby. As you fill out the worksheet, don't be alarmed if you can't determine exact amounts for last month's expenses; most people can't. If you are not sure of the amount spent in each category, try to estimate to the best of your ability. (Many people will not have to make most of the entries under the Insurance or Taxes columns because those expenditures are automatically deducted from a paycheck. If you're self-employed, though, make sure you get good estimates for those numbers.)

Peak Expenses

Once you have determined your previous month's spending, remember that the precise amount of money you need to meet your monthly expenses will actually vary from month to month. One way you can gain control over your budget is to know which months carry with them the largest expenses. Some months you will spend less than you earn, and other months you will spend far more. We all know that there are big expenses at Christmastime, or when income taxes come due, or when your children go back to school. Once you identify your peak expense periods you can match them with your peak income periods. Use the worksheet titled "Identification of Yearly Peak Expenses" at the end of this chapter or on the CD-ROM to determine these expenses.

Peak Income

Just as expenses vary from month to month, so does your income. We all love those times when we get a bonus from work, or when we get back a hefty tax refund. If you get paid on a bi-weekly basis, there will be at least two months of the year when you will have an extra paycheck. If you work on a commission basis or are self-employed, you are already acutely aware of the reality of fluctuating income. The key to controlling your money is to balance your peak income against your peak expenses, even if that means putting money aside in savings for those expensive months. Once you stop using your peak income to go on impulsive buying sprees, you will be well on the road to becoming a master of your finances. Use the worksheet titled "Identification of Yearly Peak Income" to determine the months that your income peaks. This worksheet follows the "Identification of Yearly Peak Expenses" form at the end of this chapter and on the CD-ROM.

Total Worth

Your total worth is a compilation of all your assets. Everything from savings accounts to real estate make up the total of all you are worth. You can't determine your overall financial picture until you know your total worth. You will undoubtedly have more assets than you realize. Some of the items you may consider debts, such as your house, are really assets. They are assets with an increasing value. Automobiles, clothing, appliances, and furniture are also assets, but they are assets that depreciate in value. The value of your automobile today is not the value of that same automobile a year from now. Everything you own has a value. Listing your assets helps you to evaluate and prioritize your expenses and plan for future needs. The worksheet titled "How Much Are You Worth?" will help you determine your total worth.

The next chapter will help you finish your plan by creating a tally of your yearly expenses and showing you how to use the computer to crunch your numbers and come up with a budget that works for you.

Identification of Yearly Peak Expenses

Possible peak expenses include the following:

    Car or life insurance   Fall school clothes

    Vacations   Car licenses

    Taxes   Christmas

Expense	Month Due	Est. Amount
1. _____	_____	$_____
2. _____	_____	$_____
3. _____	_____	$_____
4. _____	_____	$_____
5. _____	_____	$_____
6. _____	_____	$_____
7. _____	_____	$_____
8. _____	_____	$_____
9. _____	_____	$_____
10. _____	_____	$_____
11. _____	_____	$_____
12. _____	_____	$_____
13. _____	_____	$_____
14. _____	_____	$_____
15. _____	_____	$_____

Total Yearly Peak Expenses: $_____

Identification of Yearly Peak Income

Possible peak income sources include the following:

Dividends	Extra checks
Income tax returns	Bonus

Part-time work, second job, or freelance work

List Income Source	Month	Est. Amount
1. _____	_____	$_____
2. _____	_____	$_____
3. _____	_____	$_____
4. _____	_____	$_____
5. _____	_____	$_____
6. _____	_____	$_____
7. _____	_____	$_____
8. _____	_____	$_____
9. _____	_____	$_____
10. _____	_____	$_____
11. _____	_____	$_____
12. _____	_____	$_____
13. _____	_____	$_____
14. _____	_____	$_____
15. _____	_____	$_____

Total Yearly Peak Income: $_____

How Much Are You Worth?

Assets	Cash Value
Annuities	$_____
Art collection	$_____
Automobiles	$_____
Bonds	$_____
Cash on hand	$_____
Checking	$_____
Furs	$_____
Home (Equity)	$_____
Household furnishings	$_____
IRAs	$_____
Jewelry	$_____
KEOGH	$_____
Life insurance	$_____
Loans to others	$_____
Money market accounts	$_____
Mutual funds	$_____
Personal property	$_____
Profit sharing income	$_____
Real estate value	$_____
Small business ownership	$_____
Stocks	$_____
Other _____	$_____
Other _____	$_____
Other _____	$_____
Other _____	$_____
(A) Total Assets	$_____
(B) Total Debts	$_____
Your Total Worth*:	$_____

*Your Total Worth is your total assets minus your total debts. In addition to assets listed above you may have other retirement plans and social security benefits that could be considered part of your worth.

LAST MONTH'S INCOME AND SPENDING

Month:

Husband's Gross Income		Wife's Gross Income		Other Gross Income	

PROJECTED INCOME (TAKE HOME)

Source	Amount
Husband	
Wife	
Other	
Total	$

PROJECTED BUDGET

Expense	Amount
A. AUTO/TRANSPORTATION	
1 Bus fare	
2 Car extras	
3 Fuel (Auto #1)	
4 Fuel (Auto #2)	
5 Licenses—Fees (#1)	
6 Licenses—Fees (#2)	
7 Parking—Tolls	
8 Payment (Auto #1)	
9 Payment (Auto #2)	
10 Propane	
11 Recreation veh.	
12 Repairs (Auto #1)	
13 Repairs (Auto #2)	
14 Service (Auto #1)	
15 Service (Auto #2)	
16 Tires (Auto #1)	
17 Tires (Auto #2)	
18 Other	
19 Other	
20 **Subtotal**	$

C. CHARITY/CONTRIBUTIONS

21 Tithing	
22 Other church donations	
23 Boy Scouts	
24 United Way	
25 Other	
26 **Subtotal**	$

D. DEBTS/CREDIT CARDS

27 **Power Payment**	
28 Credit card A	
29 Credit card B	
30 Credit card C	
31 Other	
32 **Subtotal**	$

E. EDUCATION

33 Books	
34 Fees/dues	
35 Internet	
36 Lessons	
37 Magazines/newspaper	
38 Musical instruments	
39 Preschool	
40 Supplies	
41 Tuition	
42 Other	
43 **Subtotal**	$

F. FOOD

44 Dairy	
45 Eating out	
46 Food storage	

47 Groceries (incl. non-foods)
48 Junk food/beverages
49 Lunches
50 Meat
51 Special occasions
52 Other
53 Other
54 **Subtotal** | $

G. GIFTS
55 Anniversary
56 Birthdays
57 Christmas
58 Special Occasions
59 Weddings
60 Other
61 **Subtotal** | $

H. HOME/SHELTER
62 Appliances
63 Cleaning
64 Furniture
65 Garden
66 Improvements
67 Landscape
68 Mortgage
69 Mortgage (Second)
70 Rent
71 Repair
72 Other
73 Other
74 **Subtotal** | $

I. INSURANCE
75 Accident
76 Auto
77 Health
78 Home/Property
79 Life
80 Mortgage
81 Travel
82 Other
83 Other
84 **Subtotal** | $

L. LEISURE/RECREATION
85 Cable TV
86 Gym fees
87 Hobbies
88 Going out on the town
89 Toys
90 Tickets
91 Other
92 Other
93 **Subtotal** | $

M. MEDICAL
94 Dentist
95 Doctor
96 Eye care
97 Hospital
98 Prescriptions
99 Other
100 Other
101 **Subtotal** | $

O. OTHER/MISCELLANEOUS
- 102 Alimony
- 103 Baby-sitter/Daycare
- 104 Checks for cash
- 105 Children's allowances
- 106 Child support
- 107 Mad Money
- 108 Pet supplies
- 109 Postage
- 110 Other
- 111 Other
- 112 **Subtotal** $

P. PERSONALS
- 113 Hair
- 114 Makeup
- 115 Hygiene
- 116 Other
- 117 **Subtotal** $

S. SAVINGS/INVESTMENTS
- 118 Missionary savings
- 119 Rainy-day fund
- 120 Real estate or rentals
- 121 Retirement
- 122 Savings account
- 123 Stocks/Other Investments
- 124 Set aside/Christmas
- 125 Set aside/New car
- 126 Set Aside
- 127 Set Aside
- 128 **Subtotal** $

T. TAXES
- 129 Automobile
- 130 FICA (Soc. Sec.)
- 131 Federal Income
- 132 Inheritance
- 133 Property
- 134 State Income
- 135 Unemployment
- 136 Other
- 137 Other
- 138 **Subtotal** $

U. UTILITIES
- 139 Cell phone
- 140 Electricity
- 141 Garbage
- 142 Gas
- 143 Heating
- 144 Sewer
- 145 Telephone
- 146 Water
- 147 Other
- 148 **Subtotal** $

V. VACATION/TRAVEL
- 149 Food
- 150 Lodging
- 151 Souvenirs
- 152 Travel
- 153 Other
- 154 Other
- 155 **Subtotal** $

W. WARDROBE/CLOTHING

156 Cleaning—Laundry
157 Clothing—Men's
158 Clothing—Women's
159 Clothing—Children's
160 Other
161 Other
162 **Subtotal** $

SUMMARY

	Totals
INCOME	$
EXPENSES (incl. savings)	$
DIFFERENCE	$

CHAPTER 9

A Yearly and Monthly Plan

The rich ruleth over the poor, and the borrower is servant to the lender.

—PROVERBS 22:7

A maintenance plan is established after determining exactly how you *spend* your money every month. Finding yourself debt-free depends not so much on what you *earn* as it does on what you *spend*. Keeping your spending in established and planned boundaries necessitates living by a family budget.

A research organization was hired to poll a small town to find out how families spent their money. One elderly lady told the young researcher that she spent about 30 percent for shelter, 30 percent for clothing, 40 percent for food, and 20 percent for everything else. "But that adds up to 120 percent," the young man protested. "I know," she replied. "And it seems to get worse every year."

The thinking of this woman would be laughable if she didn't represent so many of us. We all know how to make money; we just don't know how to spend it.

There are some people who feel that making a plan to spend their money restricts their freedom. They refuse to make a plan.

They set off on no particular path with no particular place to go and with no way of knowing when they will get there. They'd never follow this same course in other pursuits; yet when it comes to spending money, they seem to think this is all right. This thinking does not represent you, does it?

Taking the time to plan your yearly and monthly strategy and to tally the results will reap big benefits. It will save you hundreds of dollars each year and it will make and keep you debt-free. But, be patient: With any new skill, your first attempts may not be easy to stick to. With each succeeding month and year, your skills will improve. Don't become discouraged. As you grow in experience, you will make all the adjustments necessary to your success. The principles you have learned will become so ingrained that you will no longer have to think through so many details as you plan each month's spending. Soon it will become second nature to you. How many details you will need to successfully develop a family spending plan will depend entirely on your own personality and your own method of doing things.

A spending plan is an individual thing. We have not written this book to dictate how your family ought to spend its money. We are only here to teach you some proven money management skills and then let you and your family make all the decisions as to how to spend it. *You* are in charge. *You* are in control. *You* are free to make all the decisions when it comes to spending your money. Only you can assess your own needs and wants. Over the years you will undoubtedly develop your own procedures. They will be specifically tailored to fit your own lifestyle and your own goals. Even if you've never been able to successfully budget before, this time can be different. Make it a mind-set. You can do it!

Last of all—always include some flexibility in your budget. The mistake some novices, and even the more experienced budgeters, make is that they fail to include any flexibility in their monthly plan. When a budget is too rigid, it is an invitation to disaster. No one can survive forever on an inflexible and joyless budget. Allow a cushion for unplanned expenses, as most months will have just a few; give yourself what we call Mad Money to spend any way you choose, and always allow your companion the same sort of flexibility you give yourself. Budgets are not weapons; they are guides to assist you in spending your money wisely.

Your Yearly Financial Plan

We suggest that you base your spending plan on last year's expenses and then look at the coming year in advance. Why? Because looking at an entire year in advance allows you to see periods of peak income and peak expenses and to plan for those times well in advance. This, in turn, assures that your yearly spending does not exceed your yearly income. Looking at just one month at a time is inefficient because it doesn't allow you to see that there will be months when you spend more than you earn. These months can be planned by setting aside funds in the months where you earn more than you spend. Not preparing for these months could very well mean that you find yourself in debt again. And you're trying to be debt-free, right?

Once you have established this precedent and have a year's history to reflect back on, you will be able to more easily plan next year's budget. In fact, your first year of becoming debt-free and instituting the Yearly Financial Plan outlined in this book will probably be the year with the least accurate budgeting. Once you've done this for a year, and then another year, and then another year, your yearly plan will become more and more accurate.

Additionally, there will always be expenses you did not anticipate, but generally you will know, at least a year in advance, what manner of expenses you might encounter. Write these expenses down now! Even if you don't know exact amounts, your best estimate will, at the very least, put you on the right track. As you look ahead, anticipate things like maintenance, repairs, and unusual household expenses. For example, an automobile with high mileage will probably break down once or twice in the coming year, so expect some repair costs. A fourteen-year-old washing machine might soon need to be replaced—better figure on that. Maybe this is the year to take that dream vacation, or maybe the walls of your house could use a little new paint. Even a new baby will allow you nine months to make financial preparations. Here is your chance to anticipate the needs of the upcoming year. Be sure you remember when your insurance premiums come due and when it is time to pay property and income taxes. Plan for Christmas, birthdays, and holidays. A worksheet just for this purpose is called "Things to Remember" and is included on pages 114–15 as well as on the CD-ROM. The worksheets in the previous chapter will prove very useful in identifying periods of peak income and expenses. The remaining worksheets in this chapter will provide a solid base from which you can later plan your monthly strategies.

By anticipating months in advance and building a yearly budget before your monthly plan, you will find the entire process less stressful. Planning a year in advance will keep you focused on long-range goals and eliminate the distraction and temptation of impulse buying. You will come to know that the money you have left over from one month's budget must be used to pay next month's expenses. Therefore, you will know you cannot spend it impulsively; it must be planned for.

The Dixons' Yearly Plan

Let's go back and look at how the Dixon family developed their plan. Dan and Janet began setting up a yearly strategy in

December. Since this was the first time they had planned a yearly strategy, they collected information for two weeks. This included filling out the forms titled "Last Month's Income and Spending," "Identification of Yearly Peak Income," and "Identification of Yearly Peak Expenses" from the previous chapter and recording a variety of important extra details on the "Things to Remember" worksheet included in this chapter and on the CD-ROM. After collecting the needed information, the Dixons were ready for a family council. They met just before the start of the new year.

The first thing they did was to anticipate their income for the coming year. On the form titled "Yearly Financial Plan," they input their income for each month of the year. Then, they worked to identify periods of peak income for the coming year. Dan received two $550 profit-sharing checks last year and a $1,500 income tax refund. Dan wasn't sure if the amounts would be the same for the next year, but he anticipated they would be close. The months in which he received the profit-sharing checks (May and October) and the tax refund (June) were his peak-income months.

Janet input her income as well. She didn't have any peak income months, but her supervisor had told her she would be getting a nice raise this year—somewhere in the neighborhood of $50 a month. Janet remembered that they needed to plan for a crisis if they wanted to remain debt-free, so she offered to put the amount of her raise into a rainy-day fund for unexpected expenses. By itself it wasn't much, but Janet knew it would add up nicely as each month went by, and it would be there whenever the family truly needed it. This was part of a crisis plan.

After considering their income for the year, the family began to identify their peak expenses. These included a small vacation, back-to-school funds, and an annual check up with the dentist. They penciled in the corresponding amounts on the "Things to

Remember" worksheet and decided that their profit-sharing checks and perhaps some of their income tax refund could be used for those expenses.

They also considered peak expenses that would occur years down the road. In doing so, they decided to open a mission savings account and determined that this year they could safely contribute $25 each month. Next year they hoped to increase the amount. In addition, Dan knew of at least two major expenses that could easily land them right back in debt: Christmas and a new car. The family discussed these two items for a while and decided to open two more "set-aside" savings accounts. They agreed to set aside $100 each month to split between Christmas money and a new car fund. The Dixons entered the total of all their savings ($175 per month) in the Savings/Investment row at the bottom of the "Yearly Financial Plan" form. With each number entered, the computer automatically adjusted their totals and helped them know whether or not they were using too much of their projected income.

They then used the "Things to Remember" and "Last Month's Income and Spending" forms to fill out the Projected Expenses area of the "Yearly Financial Plan." In March, for example, the Dixons came up with a total for the Auto/Transportation category by adding last month's total expenses for that category ($282) with the $135 they knew they would have to pay to register one of their cars. This made total spending for Auto/Transportation $417 in March. They put that number in the correct column on the form. They did this with every category and month on the chart. Each time, the computer adjusted the numbers to show them how much they would be spending that month. The very last row on the "Yearly Financial Plan" form showed the balance for the month. (Numbers in parentheses are amounts for which the Dixons would potentially overspend. This, however, would be okay, as long as other months helped them to balance out.)

As they developed their plan, they discovered that the money they would receive during peak-income periods left them with additional money to set aside for peak-expense periods. In June, for example, they decided they would place $700 of their estimated $1,500 tax return in their savings account. They would use $300 of that amount on Christmas expenses in December. (When added to the $50 a month they planned to save for Christmas, this gave them $900 to spend for the holiday. In December, they would move $900 into their checking account and list it as income for the month. This way, when they listed the $900 in the projected expenses column for December, it would balance out.) The remaining $400 could be split between their rainy-day funds and their mission fund. They'd keep the rest of their income tax refund ($800) in their checking account to use against a vacation and school clothes later that summer.

Even after earmarking these savings and expenses, they discovered that they would often have additional funds left over at the end of the month. These funds, which would equal approximately $650 by the year's end, would serve as a cushion for unexpected expenses. If they didn't need the $650 by year's end, they decided they would take whatever remained and also set that aside into savings. This was a part of their future plan. Once all the numbers were input, the Dixons looked over the plan. Had they had enough for a power payment? You bet they had. Look at the "Dixon Family Yearly Financial Plan" on pages 102–3. You will discover that the Dixons were able to put 10 percent of their take-home pay, $425, into a power payment to retire their debts. (You'll find this amount listed in the Debts and

THINGS TO REMEMBER—SAMPLE

Item:	Amount
JANUARY	
1 Boy Scouts	$ 25
2 Jamie's birthday	$ 30
3	
4	
5	

Item:	Amount
FEBRUARY	
1 Dan's birthday	$ 50
2 United Way	$ 15
3	
4	
5	

Item:	Amount
MARCH	
1 Jason's birthday	$ 30
2 Register auto #1	$ 135
3 Dentist	$ 250
4	
5	

Item:	Amount
APRIL	
1 Club dues	$ 25
2 Fall football tickets	$ 120
3	
4	
5	

Item:	Amount
MAY	
1 Flowers, garden, and lawn care	$ 150
2 Paint 3 rooms	$ 200
3 Register auto #2	$ 100
4 Set aside profit sharing	$ 550
5	

Item:	Amount
JUNE	
1 Janet & Jennifer's birthdays	$ 80
2 Swimming lessons	$ 30
3 Service cars	$ 40
4 Camp for boys	$ 60
5 Set aside tax refund	$ 1,500

Item:			Amount
JULY			
1 Vacation		$	400
2 Justin's birthday		$	30
3 New tires auto #1		$	250
4			
5			

Item:			Amount
AUGUST			
1 Back to school clothes		$	450
2 School fees		$	150
3			
4			
5			

Item:			Amount
SEPTEMBER			
1 Anniversary		$	60
2 Dentist		$	300
3			
4			
5			

Item:			Amount
OCTOBER			
1 Winterize cars		$	150
2 Clean carpets		$	200
3 Set aside profit sharing		$	550
4			
5			

Item:			Amount
NOVEMBER			
1			
2			
3			
4			
5			

Item:			Amount
DECEMBER			
1 Christmas		$	900
2 Transfer $900 from Christmas savings to pay			
3 for Christmas			
4			
5			

DIXON FAMILY YEARLY FINANCIAL PLAN

YEAR | 2001

PROJECTED INCOME

Sources	Jan	Feb	Mar	Apr	May	Jun
Husband	$ 3,552	$ 3,552	$ 3,552	$ 3,552	$ 3,552	$ 3,552
Wife	$ 700	$ 700	$ 700	$ 700	$ 700	$ 700
Other					$ 550	$ 1,500
Subtotal	**$ 4,252**	**$ 4,252**	**$ 4,252**	**$ 4,252**	**$ 4,802**	**$ 5,752**

PROJECTED EXPENSES

Category	Jan	Feb	Mar	Apr	May	Jun
Auto/Trans.	$ 332	$ 282	$ 417	$ 282	$ 382	$ 322
Charity	$ 586	$ 576	$ 561	$ 561	$ 616	$ 561
Debts/Credit card	$ 600	$ 600	$ 600	$ 600	$ 600	$ 600
Education	$ 45	$ 45	$ 45	$ 45	$ 45	$ 135
Food	$ 525	$ 525	$ 525	$ 610	$ 525	$ 525
Gifts	$ 30	$ 50	$ 30	$ 10	$ 5	$ 80
Home/Shelter	$ 1,018	$ 1,018	$ 1,018	$ 1,018	$ 1,368	$ 1,018
Insurance	$ 140	$ 140	$ 140	$ 140	$ 140	$ 140
Leisure	$ 60	$ 60	$ 60	$ 205	$ 60	$ 60
Medical	$ 117	$ 117	$ 367	$ 117	$ 117	$ 117
Other/Misc.	$ 40	$ 40	$ 40	$ 40	$ 40	$ 40
Personals	$ 55	$ 30	$ 30	$ 25	$ 30	$ 45
Taxes	$ 100	$ 100	$ 100	$ 100	$ 100	$ 100
Utilities	$ 335	$ 353	$ 335	$ 303	$ 253	$ 253
Vacation/Travel						
Wardrobe	$ 55	$ 55	$ 55	$ 100	$ 100	$ 100
Subtotal	**$ 4,038**	**$ 3,991**	**$ 4,323**	**$ 4,156**	**$ 4,381**	**$ 4,096**

SUMMARY OF PROJECTED FINANCES

Totals	Jan	Feb	Mar	Apr	May	Jun
Income	$ 4,252	$ 4,252	$ 4,252	$ 4,252	$ 4,802	$ 5,752
Expenses	$ 4,038	$ 3,991	$ 4,323	$ 4,156	$ 4,381	$ 4,096
Savings/Invest.	$ 175	$ 175	$ 175	$ 175	$ 175	$ 875
DIFFERENCE	**$ 39**	**$ 86**	**$ (246)**	**$ (79)**	**$ 246**	**$ 781**

	Jul	Aug	Sep	Oct	Nov	Dec	Total
$	3,552	3,552	3,552	3,552	3,552	3,552	42,624
$	700	700	700	700	700	700	8,400
$				550		900	3,500
$	4,252	4,252	4,252	4,802	4,252	5,152	54,524

	Jul	Aug	Sep	Oct	Nov	Dec	Total
$	532	282	282	432	282	282	4,109
$	561	561	561	616	561	561	6,882
$	600	600	600	600	600	600	7,200
$	45	195	45	45	45	45	780
$	525	525	525	525	610	625	6,570
$	30	5	60	5	5	900	1,210
$	1,018	1,018	1,018	1,218	1,018	1,018	12,766
$	140	140	140	140	140	140	1,680
$	60	60	60	60	60	60	865
$	117	117	417	117	117	117	1,954
$	40	40	40	40	40	40	480
$	25	30	25	30	25	30	380
$	100	100	100	100	100	100	1,200
$	253	253	253	253	298	298	3,440
$	400						400
$	55	450	100	55	30		1,155
$	4,501	4,376	4,226	4,236	3,931	4,816	51,071

	Jul	Aug	Sep	Oct	Nov	Dec	Total
$	4,252	4,252	4,252	4,802	4,252	5,152	54,524
$	4,501	4,376	4,226	4,236	3,931	4,816	51,071
$	175	175	175	175	175	175	2,800
$	(424)	(299)	(149)	391	146	161	653

Credit Cards row—it has been added to the regular monthly payments of their credit cards.) They understood the wisdom of this process and were eager to get started. They knew that some of their debts would be quickly eliminated—at least five within the first year and all but their mortgage in their second year. They also knew that as each debt was paid off, the amount they were paying monthly on that debt would be added to the power payment and be applied to the next debt. (Note that the exact amounts of the Dixons' car debt, medical debt, and homeowner's debt is included in the separate rows for those categories and not listed in the Debts and Credit Cards row. Also, the amount listed in the Debts and Credit Cards row stays the same each month— even though some of the credit cards will be paid off before the end of the year—because the total amount of money paid toward *all* debts will be the same every month if they follow the Power Payment Plan.) Not only could they plan for today but they could also plan for tomorrow and for a crisis and still have enough income to pay off their debts. It wasn't unrealistic; it was now their reality.

You can set up a yearly strategy just as Janet and Dan did. To access the "Yearly Financial Plan" worksheet, go to the main menu, click on Create a yearly and monthly budget plan, then click on the icon next to Yearly Financial Plan. The computer will total your numbers for you.

Keep expenses low enough to save that 10 to 15 percent needed to put toward the elimination of your debts. Give yourself a cushion against unexpected expenses. If you have kept last year's checks, look them over. Do you see any expenses you didn't antici-pate—Boy Scout Registration, PTA fund-raisers, school fees, church donations? Add these to your "Things to Remember" list.

Your Monthly Plan

Once you've established a plan for spending your money a year in advance, it will be a little easier to establish a monthly plan. You will remember that some months will be more expensive and that other months will be less; yet you will know that the money will be available when you need it to meet all your needs and to eliminate your debts. As you plan for each month's spending, refer back to your year's plan and follow the guidelines you have established. We'll go back to the Dixon family to show you how a typical monthly planning session would work.

The Dixons' Monthly Plan

Dan and Janet brought their whole family together to set up their monthly budget. It was the second day of the month, so they were getting a head start. They didn't want to start spending the month's money without first establishing a plan. It was their goal to meet in a family council within the first three days of the month. To get ready, Janet put all the bills in an envelope and wrote down any known expenses before they met. Dan looked over the yearly plan to see if any expenses had been overlooked. It was then that he remembered that their home insurance needed to be accounted for so he decided to budget $40 a month to cover it when it came due. Now Dan and Janet were ready to include their children in their plan.

Dan and Janet used the form titled "The Plan," which is at the end of this chapter and on the CD-ROM, as the base for their monthly budget. As they came to each category on the form, they asked their children if they knew of any expenses they would have in that category. Justin needed new notebook paper for school. They added the cost of that under education. Jason, who was in the third grade, wanted to buy some books in his next "book order" from the school. He wanted $10 worth of books, but they allowed him $5. He wasn't happy, but he lived with it. It was Jamie's birthday that month, and to meet their power payment they allowed a $30 limit for her gifts as they would do with all their children when their birthdays came around. Dan agreed to sacrifice by taking the bus to work every day, saving the money that would have been spent on fuel for his car. The give and take went on as Dan and Janet, along with their children, adjusted their monthly expenses to meet their income.

The Plan and the Tally

At the end of the chapter and on the CD-ROM you will find charts to assist you and your family as you plan and tally your monthly expenses.

The worksheet titled "The Plan" allows you to project or budget for each upcoming month. Always begin by consulting your yearly strategy and actual results from the month before. Record the amounts of your projected bills and consult your calendar to see if upcoming events may carry expenses with them. For example, an upcoming trip to visit your parents in another city will carry with it some expenses, which you can anticipate and plan for in advance.

If you use the computer program, subtotals from "The Plan" worksheet will be automatically carried over to the appropriate line on "The Tally" worksheet. With projected budgets in each category, you will have a weekly tally to assess where you are with your spending. "The Tally" worksheet is designed to deduct your actual expenses from your projected budget so that you always know how much remains in each budgeted category.

"The Plan"

The categories we have designed for planning your budget are based on a mnemonic system. Each category starts with a letter of the alphabet to make it easier for you to remember and to track. Here are the categories we will use to set up your monthly plan:

A = Auto and Transportation
C = Charity and Contributions
D = Debt and Credit Cards
E = Education
F = Food
G = Gifts
H = Home and Shelter
I = Insurance
L = Leisure and Recreation
M = Medical
O = Other/Miscellaneous
P = Personals
S = Savings and Investments
T = Taxes
U = Utilities
V = Vacation/Travel
W = Wardrobe/Clothing

Monthly plans are a day-to-day philosophy. It will probably take you three months before you start seeing any real success. The first month must allow for failure time. You are embarking on something new and different. You will likely fall short of your goals to some extent, because you will be getting a bearing on your finances. This is the time for you to remember to not be discouraged. You'll improve with each passing month. The second month is likely to be an adjustment time. You will still be a little soft in adjusting to your budget from the month before, but control will come. The third month will mark your successful beginning. By the third month most people's budgets will be fairly accurate. Of course, there will always be surprises, but you will learn to adjust for them. Remember to take it a day at a time. Everyone fails now and again—even months down the road you'll make mistakes, but you will also learn to deal with your failures and to make adjustments for them.

Instructions

You may use "The Plan" worksheet at the end of the chapter or you may use the computer template included on the CD-ROM. Either choice will work; however, the computer program will do all the calculations for you. Remember that in order to *pay off your debts*, your original goal, you should include in your plan a 10 to 15 percent power payment. This is one of the first figures you will want to compute into your monthly plan. To access a worksheet for each month, go to the main menu, click on Create a yearly and monthly budget plan, then select the month you'd like to budget.

"The Plan" should be developed within the first three days of the month. It does little good to plan after the fact. Be sure to consult the yearly financial plan and record any pertinent data.

Try to achieve your financial objectives in small doses. Try to find a dollar here and a dollar there.

The first step will be to fill in your projected income. This amount is fixed if you receive a standard paycheck, but for some, your income may vary from month to month because you are self-employed or have an occupation with fluctuations in pay. If you fall into this variable category you can estimate your income to the best of your ability. Records from previous years can give you a fairly good idea of what you might reasonably expect. Do the best you can. After a year of working with your monthly plan, you will probably get fairly accurate at predicting income.

Now, fill in the projected expenses. There are two kinds of expenses: *fixed expenses* and *discretionary expenses*. Fixed expenses are known and easy to anticipate. They include car payments, mortgage payments, debt payments of any kind, taxes, and utility bills. Yet, even some fixed expenses can be trimmed. At the end of this book we've listed simple ways to save in every budget category—including those that seem to be fixed. "Discretionary expenses" vary from month to month. These expenses offer you the most flexibility in your budget. Use the "Last Month's Income and Spending" worksheet (pages 89–92) to assist you in finding reasonable totals.

The Tally

"The Tally" worksheet will help you keep track of your actual expenses. "The Tally" should be done each week, preferably on the same day and at the same time. Being consistent is the key to success. We've told you that many families use Saturday mornings to tally their expenses. More money is spent on weekends than any other time. Saturday may be the best time for a family just beginning to plan for their expenses. However, you may find that some other day works better for you. The time you choose is not as important as the principle of establishing a scheduled time. This should take you only about a half hour per week and it may be the most vital half hour you spend. Married couples should do their tally together. They need to remain united to be successful at not only managing money but at becoming debt-free. Single parents with children might consider having their older children help them. But single or married, parents need the support of children to make their plan work. Children need not necessarily be involved with every tally session, but they should be involved in the planning and ought to see the ending tally to assess how well their family is doing. When families are committed to being debt-free, squabbles over money diminish and may even disappear.

That brings us to our most important point. Tallying time is not a time to bicker. When mistakes are made, and they will be, don't affix blame, just admit the mistake, try to do better, and move on. Next week will be different. There is always a period of adjustment before you'll reach anticipated results.

Instructions

Each week, as you meet to record your tally, follow these instructions. To access The Tally, go to the main menu, click on Create a tally of your daily activity, then select the month for which you'd like to record your data.

Record actual expenses under the appropriate category and day of the month. To make this easier you will find the expense categories are listed in mnemonics (alphabetical codes): "A" for auto, "W" for wardrobe, and so on. The days of the month are listed 1 through 31.

Record cash, check, and credit card purchases.

When you have input your purchases, the template will automatically deduct it from your budget totals. The template will tell you how much remains in each budget category.

If you start to run over in a category, go back and look carefully at your spending. Try to assess where you are having problems. Adjust expenses for next week. When it's impossible to adjust weekly expenses, make notes on the "Things to Remember" worksheet and adjust next month's or next year's budget.

Amounts left at the end of the month can be carried over to meet peak expenses in upcoming months, or they can be set aside into savings accounts.

Yearly Record

There is one more worksheet needed to complete the maintenance plan. This is the yearly record. Here is how it works: At the end of each month, transfer the total expenses of each category from your tally to the "Yearly Record of Finances." Be sure to remember to record any unplanned expenses. This history will form the basis of next year's budget, so transferring this information is essential. If you're using the computerized worksheets, you won't have to transfer any numbers. As you fill out The Tally, the numbers will be transferred automatically.

For the Dixons, the yearly record allowed them to see how well they were doing. They were surprised at how successful they had been. At first it had been difficult to stick with their plan, but as the year wore on, Janet and Dan were surprised at how much further their money stretched. When the car broke down in June, they only had to withdraw $150 from the rainy-day fund to cover the $350 repair. They were doing even better than they expected. Janet and Dan found that with proper planning, peak income could cover periods of peak expense. Their key was to keep the cash flow as level as possible. In fact, after just six months of adhering to their plan, Janet told Dan that she could not even detect a change in their lifestyle. She had thought they were tightening their belts when they started, but she found that they were living just as well as they had the year previous— except that they were no longer sinking deeper in debt and they never fought about money anymore.

YEARLY FINANCIAL PLAN

YEAR [　　　　　]

PROJECTED INCOME

Sources	Jan	Feb	Mar	Apr	May	Jun
Husband						
Wife						
Other						
Subtotal	$	$	$	$	$	$

PROJECTED EXPENSES

Category	Jan	Feb	Mar	Apr	May	Jun
Auto/Trans.						
Charity						
Debts/Credit card						
Education						
Food						
Gifts						
Home/Shelter						
Insurance						
Leisure						
Medical						
Other/Misc.						
Personals						
Taxes						
Utilities						
Vacation/Travel						
Wardrobe						
Subtotal	$	$	$	$	$	$

SUMMARY OF PROJECTED FINANCES

Totals	Jan	Feb	Mar	Apr	May	Jun
Income						
Expenses						
Savings/Invest.						
DIFFERENCE	$	$	$	$	$	$

Jul	Aug	Sep	Oct	Nov	Dec	Total
						$
						$
						$
$	$	$	$	$	$	$

Jul	Aug	Sep	Oct	Nov	Dec	Total
						$
						$
						$
						$
						$
						$
						$
						$
						$
						$
						$
						$
						$
						$
						$
						$
$	$	$	$	$	$	$

Jul	Aug	Sep	Oct	Nov	Dec	Total
						$
						$
						$
$	$	$	$	$	$	$

THINGS TO REMEMBER

Item: Amount
                        JANUARY
1 _____
2 _____
3 _____
4 _____
5 _____

Item: Amount
                        FEBRUARY
1 _____
2 _____
3 _____
4 _____
5 _____

Item: Amount
                        MARCH
1 _____
2 _____
3 _____
4 _____
5 _____

Item: Amount
                        APRIL
1 _____
2 _____
3 _____
4 _____
5 _____

Item: Amount
                        MAY
1 _____
2 _____
3 _____
4 _____
5 _____

Item: Amount
                        JUNE
1 _____
2 _____
3 _____
4 _____
5 _____

Item: JULY   Amount

1
2
3
4
5

Item: AUGUST   Amount

1
2
3
4
5

Item: SEPTEMBER   Amount

1
2
3
4
5

Item: OCTOBER   Amount

1
2
3
4
5

Item: NOVEMBER   Amount

1
2
3
4
5

Item: DECEMBER   Amount

1
2
3
4
5

THE PLAN—SAMPLE

Month: January

Husband's Gross Income	Wife's Gross Income	Other Gross Income
$ 4,510.00	$ 800.00	

PROJECTED INCOME (TAKE HOME)

Source	Amount
Husband	$ 3,552
Wife	$ 700
Other	
Total	**$ 4,252**

PROJECTED BUDGET

Expense	Amount
A. AUTO/TRANSPORTATION	
1 Bus fare	
2 Car extras	
3 Fuel (Auto #1)	$ 60
4 Fuel (Auto #2)	$ 20
5 Licenses—Fees (#1)	
6 Licenses—Fees (#2)	
7 Parking—Tolls	
8 Payment (Auto #1)	$ 202
9 Payment (Auto #2)	
10 Propane	
11 Recreation veh.	
12 Repairs (Auto #1)	$ 50
13 Repairs (Auto #2)	
14 Service (Auto #1)	
15 Service (Auto #2)	
16 Tires (Auto #1)	
17 Tires (Auto #2)	
18 Other	
19 Other	
20 **Subtotal**	**$ 332**

C. CHARITY/CONTRIBUTIONS

21 Tithing	$ 531
22 Other church donations	$ 30
23 Boy Scouts	$ 25
24 United Way	
25 Other	
26 **Subtotal**	**$ 586**

D. DEBTS/CREDIT CARDS

27 **Power Payment**	**$ 425**
28 Credit card A	$ 25
29 Credit card B	$ 74
30 Credit card C	$ 76
31 Other	
32 **Subtotal**	**$ 600**

E. EDUCATION

33 Books	
34 Fees/dues	
35 Internet	$ 10
36 Lessons	$ 20
37 Magazines/newspaper	$ 10
38 Musical instruments	
39 Preschool	
40 Supplies	$ 5
41 Tuition	
42 Other	
43 **Subtotal**	**$ 45**

F. FOOD

44 Dairy	
45 Eating out	$ 30
46 Food storage	$ 25

47 Groceries (incl. non-foods)	$	420
48 Junk food/beverages		
49 Lunches	$	50
50 Meat		
51 Special occasions		
52 Other		
53 Other		
54 **Subtotal**	$	**525**

G. GIFTS

55 Anniversary		
56 Birthdays	$	30
57 Christmas		
58 Special Occasions		
59 Weddings		
60 Other		
61 **Subtotal**	$	**30**

H. HOME/SHELTER

62 Appliances		
63 Cleaning		
64 Furniture		
65 Garden		
66 Improvements		
67 Landscape		
68 Mortgage	$	891
69 Mortgage (Second)	$	77
70 Rent		
71 Repair	$	50
72 Other		
73 Other		
74 **Subtotal**	$	**1,018**

I. INSURANCE

75 Accident		
76 Auto	$	100
77 Health		
78 Home/Property	$	40
79 Life		
80 Mortgage		
81 Travel		
82 Other		
83 Other		
84 **Subtotal**	$	**140**

L. LEISURE/RECREATION

85 Cable TV	$	30
86 Gym fees		
87 Hobbies		
88 Going out on the town	$	30
89 Toys		
90 Tickets		
91 Other		
92 Other		
93 **Subtotal**	$	**60**

M. MEDICAL

94 Dentist	$	62
95 Doctor	$	25
96 Eye care		
97 Hospital		
98 Prescriptions	$	30
99 Other		
100 Other		
101 **Subtotal**	$	**117**

THE PLAN—SAMPLE (continued)

O. OTHER/MISCELLANEOUS

102 Alimony		
103 Baby-sitter/Daycare		
104 Checks for cash		
105 Children's allowances		
106 Child support		
107 Mad Money	$	25
108 Pet supplies	$	5
109 Postage	$	10
110 Other		
111 Other		
112 **Subtotal**	$	**40**

P. PERSONALS

113 Hair	$	30
114 Makeup	$	15
115 Hygiene	$	10
116 Other		
117 **Subtotal**	$	**55**

S. SAVINGS/INVESTMENTS

118 Missionary savings	$	25
119 Rainy-day fund	$	50
120 Real estate or rentals		
121 Retirement		
122 Savings account		
123 Stocks/Other Investments		
124 Set aside/Christmas	$	50
125 Set aside/New car	$	50
126 Set Aside		
127 Set Aside		
128 **Subtotal**	$	**175**

T. TAXES

129 Automobile		
130 FICA (Soc. Sec.)		
131 Federal Income		
132 Inheritance		
133 Property	$	100
134 State Income		
135 Unemployment		
136 Other		
137 Other		
138 **Subtotal**	$	**100**

U. UTILITIES

139 Cell phone	$	53
140 Electricity	$	95
141 Garbage		
142 Gas	$	100
143 Heating		
144 Sewer		
145 Telephone	$	45
146 Water	$	42
147 Other		
148 **Subtotal**	$	**335**

V. VACATION/TRAVEL

149 Food		
150 Lodging		
151 Souvenirs		
152 Travel		
153 Other		
154 Other		
155 **Subtotal**	$	**-**

W. WARDROBE/CLOTHING

156 Cleaning—Laundry	$	25
157 Clothing—Men's		
158 Clothing—Women's		
159 Clothing—Children's	$	30
160 Other		
161 Other		
162 **Subtotal**	**$**	**55**

SUMMARY

	Totals	
INCOME	$	4,252
EXPENSES (incl. savings)	$	4,213
DIFFERENCE	$	39

THE PLAN

Month: [ ]

Husband's Gross Income [ ] Wife's Gross Income [ ] Other Gross Income [ ]

PROJECTED INCOME (TAKE HOME)

Source	Amount
Husband	
Wife	
Other	
Total	$

PROJECTED BUDGET

Expense	Amount
A. AUTO/TRANSPORTATION	
1 Bus fare	
2 Car extras	
3 Fuel (Auto #1)	
4 Fuel (Auto #2)	
5 Licenses—Fees (#1)	
6 Licenses—Fees (#2)	
7 Parking—Tolls	
8 Payment (Auto #1)	
9 Payment (Auto #2)	
10 Propane	
11 Recreation veh.	
12 Repairs (Auto #1)	
13 Repairs (Auto #2)	
14 Service (Auto #1)	
15 Service (Auto #2)	
16 Tires (Auto #1)	
17 Tires (Auto #2)	
18 Other	
19 Other	
20 Subtotal	$

C. CHARITY/CONTRIBUTIONS

21 Tithing	
22 Other church donations	
23 Boy Scouts	
24 United Way	
25 Other	
26 Subtotal	$

D. DEBTS/CREDIT CARDS

27 Power Payment	
28 Credit card A	
29 Credit card B	
30 Credit card C	
31 Other	
32 Subtotal	$

E. EDUCATION

33 Books	
34 Fees/dues	
35 Internet	
36 Lessons	
37 Magazines/newspaper	
38 Musical instruments	
39 Preschool	
40 Supplies	
41 Tuition	
42 Other	
43 Subtotal	$

F. FOOD

44 Dairy	
45 Eating out	
46 Food storage	

47 Groceries (incl. non-foods)
48 Junk food/beverages
49 Lunches
50 Meat
51 Special occasions
52 Other
53 Other
54 **Subtotal** $

G. GIFTS
55 Anniversary
56 Birthdays
57 Christmas
58 Special Occasions
59 Weddings
60 Other
61 **Subtotal** $

H. HOME/SHELTER
62 Appliances
63 Cleaning
64 Furniture
65 Garden
66 Improvements
67 Landscape
68 Mortgage
69 Mortgage (Second)
70 Rent
71 Repair
72 Other
73 Other
74 **Subtotal** $

I. INSURANCE
75 Accident
76 Auto
77 Health
78 Home/Property
79 Life
80 Mortgage
81 Travel
82 Other
83 Other
84 **Subtotal** $

L. LEISURE/RECREATION
85 Cable TV
86 Gym fees
87 Hobbies
88 Going out on the town
89 Toys
90 Tickets
91 Other
92 Other
93 **Subtotal** $

M. MEDICAL
94 Dentist
95 Doctor
96 Eye care
97 Hospital
98 Prescriptions
99 Other
100 Other
101 **Subtotal** $

THE PLAN (continued)

O. OTHER/MISCELLANEOUS
102 Alimony
103 Baby-sitter/Daycare
104 Checks for cash
105 Children's allowances
106 Child support
107 Mad Money
108 Pet supplies
109 Postage
110 Other
111 Other
112 **Subtotal** $

P. PERSONALS
113 Hair
114 Makeup
115 Hygiene
116 Other
117 **Subtotal** $

S. SAVINGS/INVESTMENTS
118 Missionary savings
119 Rainy-day fund
120 Real estate or rentals
121 Retirement
122 Savings account
123 Stocks/Other Investments
124 Set aside/Christmas
125 Set aside/New car
126 Set Aside
127 Set Aside
128 **Subtotal** $

T. TAXES
129 Automobile
130 FICA (Soc. Sec.)
131 Federal Income
132 Inheritance
133 Property
134 State Income
135 Unemployment
136 Other
137 Other
138 **Subtotal** $

U. UTILITIES
139 Cell phone
140 Electricity
141 Garbage
142 Gas
143 Heating
144 Sewer
145 Telephone
146 Water
147 Other
148 **Subtotal** $

V. VACATION/TRAVEL
149 Food
150 Lodging
151 Souvenirs
152 Travel
153 Other
154 Other
155 **Subtotal** $

W. WARDROBE/CLOTHING

156 Cleaning—Laundry	
157 Clothing—Men's	
158 Clothing—Women's	
159 Clothing—Children's	
160 Other	
161 Other	
162 **Subtotal**	$

SUMMARY

	Totals
INCOME	$
EXPENSES (incl. savings)	$
DIFFERENCE	$

THE TALLY—SAMPLE

AUTO/TRANSPORTATION

BUDGET:		332.00
Date	Ck.# or Cash	Amount
1	101	22.50
2	102	12.50
3		
4		
5		
6		
7		
Week 1 total		35.00
Budget Balance		**297.00**
8	118	20.08
9		
10		
11		
12		
13		
14		
Week 2 total		20.08
Budget Balance		**276.92**
15	132	22.95
16	133	202.00
17		
18		
19		
20		
21		
Week 3 total		224.95
Budget Balance		**51.97**
22	144	49.50
23		
24		
25		
26		
27		
28		
Week 4 total		49.50
Budget Balance		**2.47**
29		
30		
31		
Week 5 total		-
Budget Balance		**2.47**
Total Expenses		**329.53**

CHARITY/CONTRIBUTIONS

BUDGET:		586.00
Ck.# or Cash		Amount
103		30.00
		30.00
		556.00
119		25.00
		25.00
		531.00
		-
		531.00
145		531.00
		531.00
		-
		-
		-
Total Exps.		**586.00**

DEBTS/CREDIT CARDS

Date	Ck.# or Cash	Amount	
BUDGET:		**600.00**	
Date	Ck.# or Cash	Amount	
1	103	425.00	
2	104	25.02	
3	105	74.22	
4	106	75.50	
5			
6			
7			
Week 1 total		599.74	
Budget Balance		**0.26**	
8			
9			
10			
11			
12			
13			
14			
Week 2 total		-	
Budget Balance		**0.26**	
15			
16			
17			
18			
19			
20			
21			
Week 3 total		-	
Budget Balance		**0.26**	
22			
23			
24			
25			
26			
27			
28			
Week 4 total		-	
Budget Balance		**0.26**	
29			
30			
31			
Week 5 total		-	
Budget Balance		**0.26**	
Total Expenses		**599.74**	

EDUCATION

Ck.# or Cash	Amount	
BUDGET:	**45.00**	
Ck.# or Cash	Amount	
107	4.98	
	4.98	
	40.02	
120	20.00	
	20.00	
	20.02	
134	10.00	
	10.00	
	10.02	
146	10.00	
	10.00	
	0.02	
	-	
	0.02	
Total Exps.	**44.98**	

THE TALLY—SAMPLE (continued)

FOOD

BUDGET:		525.00	
Date	Ck.# or Cash	Amount	
1	108	39.06	
2	109	101.57	
3	110	18.99	
4	111	19.00	
5	117	25.37	
6			
7			
Week 1 total		203.99	
Budget Balance		**321.01**	
8	121	26.97	
9	122	43.74	
10	123	19.64	
11	124	29.00	
12			
13			
14			
Week 2 total		119.35	
Budget Balance		**201.66**	
15	135	38.95	
16	136	22.00	
17	137	29.00	
18			
19			
20			
21			
Week 3 total		89.95	
Budget Balance		**111.71**	
22	147	41.48	
23	148	22.00	
24	149	48.06	
25			
26			
27			
28			
Week 4 total		111.54	
Budget Balance		**0.17**	
29			
30			
31			
Week 5 total		-	
Budget Balance		**0.17**	
Total Expenses		**524.83**	

GIFTS

BUDGET:		30.00
Ck.# or Cash	Amount	
		-
		30.00
125	28.36	
		28.36
		1.64
		1.64
		-
		1.64
		-
		1.64
Total Exps.		**28.36**

HOME/SHELTER

BUDGET:		1,018.00
Date	Ck.# or Cash	Amount
1	112	891.00
2		
3		
4		
5		
6		
7		
Week 1 total		891.00
Budget Balance		127.00
8	126	44.49
9		
10		
11		
12		
13		
14		
Week 2 total		44.49
Budget Balance		82.51
15	138	77.00
16		
17		
18		
19		
20		
21		
Week 3 total		77.00
Budget Balance		5.51
22		
23		
24		
25		
26		
27		
28		
Week 4 total		-
Budget Balance		5.51
29		
30		
31		
Week 5 total		-
Budget Balance		5.51
Total Expenses		1,012.49

INSURANCE

BUDGET:		140.00
Ck.# or Cash	Amount	
	-	
	140.00	
	-	
	140.00	
	-	
	140.00	
150	100.00	
156	40.00	
	140.00	
	-	
	-	
	-	
Total Exps.	140.00	

THE TALLY—SAMPLE (continued)

LEISURE/RECREATION

Date	Ck.# or Cash	Amount	
BUDGET:			**60.00**
1			
2			
3			
4			
5			
6			
7			
Week 1 total			-
Budget Balance			**60.00**
8			
9			
10			
11			
12			
13			
14			
Week 2 total			-
Budget Balance			**60.00**
15	139	25.63	
16			
17			
18			
19			
20			
21			
Week 3 total			25.63
Budget Balance			**34.37**
22	157	29.97	
23			
24			
25			
26			
27			
28			
Week 4 total			29.97
Budget Balance			**4.40**
29			
30			
31			
Week 5 total			-
Budget Balance			**4.40**
Total Expenses			**55.60**

MEDICAL

Ck.# or Cash	Amount	
BUDGET:		**117.00**
113	10.00	
114	25.10	
		35.10
		81.90
127	15.56	
		15.56
		66.34
140	62.50	
		62.50
		3.84
		-
		3.84
		-
		3.84
Total Exps.		**113.16**

OTHER/MISCELLANEOUS

	BUDGET:	40.00
Date	Ck.# or Cash	Amount
1	115	3.98
2		
3		
4		
5		
6		
7		
Week 1 total		3.98
Budget Balance		36.02
8	128	12.80
9		
10		
11		
12		
13		
14		
Week 2 total		12.80
Budget Balance		23.22
15	141	19.31
16		
17		
18		
19		
20		
21		
Week 3 total		19.31
Budget Balance		3.91
22		
23		
24		
25		
26		
27		
28		
Week 4 total		-
Budget Balance		3.91
29		
30		
31		
Week 5 total		-
Budget Balance		3.91
Total Expenses		36.09

PERSONALS

BUDGET:	55.00
Ck.# or Cash	Amount
116	20.00
	20.00
	35.00
129	9.95
	9.95
	25.05
142	12.00
	12.00
	13.05
	-
	13.05
157	8.86
	8.86
	4.19
Total Exps.	50.81

THE TALLY—SAMPLE (continued)

SAVINGS/INVESTMENTS

Date	Ck.# or Cash	Amount	
BUDGET:		**175.00**	
Date	Ck.# or Cash	Amount	
1	TXFR Savings	125.00	
2			
3			
4			
5			
6			
7			
Week 1 total		125.00	
Budget Balance		**50.00**	
8			
9			
10			
11			
12			
13			
14			
Week 2 total		-	
Budget Balance		**50.00**	
15	TXFR Savings	50.00	
16			
17			
18			
19			
20			
21			
Week 3 total		50.00	
Budget Balance		**-**	
22			
23			
24			
25			
26			
27			
28			
Week 4 total		-	
Budget Balance		**-**	
29			
30			
31			
Week 5 total		-	
Budget Balance		**-**	
Total Expenses		**175.00**	

TAXES

Ck.# or Cash	Amount	
BUDGET:	**100.00**	
Ck.# or Cash	Amount	
	-	
	100.00	
	-	
	100.00	
	-	
	100.00	
158	100.00	
	100.00	
	-	
	-	
	-	
Total Exps.	**100.00**	

UTILITIES

	BUDGET:	335.00
Date	Ck.# or Cash	Amount
1		
2		
3		
4		
5		
6		
7		
Week 1 total		-
Budget Balance		**335.00**
8		
9		
10		
11		
12		
13		
14		
Week 2 total		-
Budget Balance		**335.00**
15		
16		
17		
18		
19		
20		
21		
Week 3 total		-
Budget Balance		**335.00**
22	151	93.65
23	152	101.20
24	153	44.80
25	154	42.00
26	159	52.89
27		
28		
Week 4 total		334.54
Budget Balance		**0.46**
29		
30		
31		
Week 5 total		-
Budget Balance		**0.46**
Total Expenses		**334.54**

VACATION/TRAVEL

BUDGET:	
Ck.# or Cash	Amount
	-
	-
	-
	-
	-
	-
	-
	-
	-
	-
Total Exps.	-

THE TALLY—SAMPLE (continued)

WARDROBE/CLOTHING		
BUDGET:		**55.00**
Date	Ck.# or Cash	Amount
1		
2		
3		
4		
5		
6		
7		
Week 1 total		-
Budget Balance		**55.00**
8	130	15.80
9		
10		
11		
12		
13		
14		
Week 2 total		15.80
Budget Balance		**39.20**
15		
16		
17		
18		
19		
20		
21		
Week 3 total		-
Budget Balance		**39.20**
22	155	33.53
23		
24		
25		
26		
27		
28		
Week 4 total		33.53
Budget Balance		**5.67**
29		
30		
31		
Week 5 total		-
Budget Balance		**5.67**
Total Expenses		**49.33**

INCOME SUMMARY		
PROJECTED		**4,252.00**
Dp.# or Cash		Amount
225		1,776.00
Subtotal		1,776.00
226		700.00
Subtotal		700.00
227		1,776.00
Subtotal		1,776.00
Subtotal		-
Subtotal		-
Total Income		**4,252.00**

SUMMARY	
INCOME	4,252.00
EXPENSES	4,180.46
DIFFERENCE	71.54
PROJECTED EXPENSES	4,213.00

THE TALLY

AUTO/TRANSPORTATION

BUDGET:		
Date	Ck.# or Cash	Amount
1		
2		
3		
4		
5		
6		
7		
Week 1 total		
Budget Balance		
8		
9		
10		
11		
12		
13		
14		
Week 2 total		
Budget Balance		
15		
16		
17		
18		
19		
20		
21		
Week 3 total		
Budget Balance		
22		
23		
24		
25		
26		
27		
28		
Week 4 total		
Budget Balance		
29		
30		
31		
Week 5 total		
Budget Balance		
Total Expenses		

CHARITY/CONTRIBUTIONS

BUDGET:	
Ck.# or Cash	Amount
Total Exps.	

THE TALLY (continued)

DEBTS/CREDIT CARDS

BUDGET:		
Date	Ck.# or Cash	Amount
1		
2		
3		
4		
5		
6		
7		
Week 1 total		
Budget Balance		
8		
9		
10		
11		
12		
13		
14		
Week 2 total		
Budget Balance		
15		
16		
17		
18		
19		
20		
21		
Week 3 total		
Budget Balance		
22		
23		
24		
25		
26		
27		
28		
Week 4 total		
Budget Balance		
29		
30		
31		
Week 5 total		
Budget Balance		
Total Expenses		

EDUCATION

BUDGET:	
Ck.# or Cash	Amount
Total Exps.	

FOOD

Date	Ck.# or Cash	Amount
BUDGET:		
1		
2		
3		
4		
5		
6		
7		
Week 1 total		
Budget Balance		
8		
9		
10		
11		
12		
13		
14		
Week 2 total		
Budget Balance		
15		
16		
17		
18		
19		
20		
21		
Week 3 total		
Budget Balance		
22		
23		
24		
25		
26		
27		
28		
Week 4 total		
Budget Balance		
29		
30		
31		
Week 5 total		
Budget Balance		
Total Expenses		

GIFTS

Ck.# or Cash	Amount
BUDGET:	
Total Exps.	

THE TALLY (continued)

HOME/SHELTER

BUDGET:		
Date	Ck.# or Cash	Amount
1		
2		
3		
4		
5		
6		
7		
Week 1 total		
Budget Balance		
8		
9		
10		
11		
12		
13		
14		
Week 2 total		
Budget Balance		
15		
16		
17		
18		
19		
20		
21		
Week 3 total		
Budget Balance		
22		
23		
24		
25		
26		
27		
28		
Week 4 total		
Budget Balance		
29		
30		
31		
Week 5 total		
Budget Balance		
Total Expenses		

INSURANCE

BUDGET:	
Ck.# or Cash	Amount
Total Exps.	

LEISURE/RECREATION

BUDGET:		
Date	Ck.# or Cash	Amount
1		
2		
3		
4		
5		
6		
7		
Week 1 total		
Budget Balance		
8		
9		
10		
11		
12		
13		
14		
Week 2 total		
Budget Balance		
15		
16		
17		
18		
19		
20		
21		
Week 3 total		
Budget Balance		
22		
23		
24		
25		
26		
27		
28		
Week 4 total		
Budget Balance		
29		
30		
31		
Week 5 total		
Budget Balance		
Total Expenses		

MEDICAL

BUDGET:	
Ck.# or Cash	Amount
Total Exps.	

THE TALLY (continued)

OTHER/MISCELLANEOUS

BUDGET:		
Date	Ck.# or Cash	Amount
1		
2		
3		
4		
5		
6		
7		
Week 1 total		
Budget Balance		
8		
9		
10		
11		
12		
13		
14		
Week 2 total		
Budget Balance		
15		
16		
17		
18		
19		
20		
21		
Week 3 total		
Budget Balance		
22		
23		
24		
25		
26		
27		
28		
Week 4 total		
Budget Balance		
29		
30		
31		
Week 5 total		
Budget Balance		
Total Expenses		

PERSONALS

BUDGET:	
Ck.# or Cash	Amount
Week 1 total	
Budget Balance	
Week 2 total	
Budget Balance	
Week 3 total	
Budget Balance	
Week 4 total	
Budget Balance	
Week 5 total	
Budget Balance	
Total Exps.	

SAVINGS/INVESTMENTS

Date	Ck.# or Cash	Amount
BUDGET:		
1		
2		
3		
4		
5		
6		
7		
Week 1 total		
Budget Balance		
8		
9		
10		
11		
12		
13		
14		
Week 2 total		
Budget Balance		
15		
16		
17		
18		
19		
20		
21		
Week 3 total		
Budget Balance		
22		
23		
24		
25		
26		
27		
28		
Week 4 total		
Budget Balance		
29		
30		
31		
Week 5 total		
Budget Balance		
Total Expenses		

TAXES

Ck.# or Cash	Amount
BUDGET:	
Total Exps.	

THE TALLY (continued)

UTILITIES

BUDGET:			
Date	Ck.# or Cash	Amount	
1			
2			
3			
4			
5			
6			
7			
Week 1 total			
Budget Balance			
8			
9			
10			
11			
12			
13			
14			
Week 2 total			
Budget Balance			
15			
16			
17			
18			
19			
20			
21			
Week 3 total			
Budget Balance			
22			
23			
24			
25			
26			
27			
28			
Week 4 total			
Budget Balance			
29			
30			
31			
Week 5 total			
Budget Balance			
Total Expenses			

VACATION/TRAVEL

BUDGET:		
Ck.# or Cash	Amount	
Total Exps.		

WARDROBE/CLOTHING

Date	Ck.# or Cash	Amount	
BUDGET:			
1			
2			
3			
4			
5			
6			
7			
Week 1 total			
Budget Balance			
8			
9			
10			
11			
12			
13			
14			
Week 2 total			
Budget Balance			
15			
16			
17			
18			
19			
20			
21			
Week 3 total			
Budget Balance			
22			
23			
24			
25			
26			
27			
28			
Week 4 total			
Budget Balance			
29			
30			
31			
Week 5 total			
Budget Balance			
Total Expenses			

INCOME SUMMARY

Dp.# or Cash	Amount	
PROJECTED		
Subtotal		
Subtotal		
Subtotal		
Subtotal		
Subtotal		
Total Income		

SUMMARY

INCOME	
EXPENSES	
DIFFERENCE	
PROJECTED EXPENSES	

YEARLY RECORD OF FINANCES

YEAR [   ]

ACTUAL INCOME

Sources	Jan	Feb	Mar	Apr	May	Jun
Husband						
Wife						
Other						
Subtotal	$	$	$	$	$	$

ACTUAL EXPENSES

Category	Jan	Feb	Mar	Apr	May	Jun
Auto/Trans.						
Charity						
Debts/Credit card						
Education						
Food						
Gifts						
Home/Shelter						
Insurance						
Leisure						
Medical						
Other/Misc.						
Personals						
Taxes						
Utilities						
Vacation/Travel						
Wardrobe						
Subtotal	$	$	$	$	$	$

SUMMARY OF FINANCES

Totals	Jan	Feb	Mar	Apr	May	Jun
Income						
Expenses						
Savings/Invest.						
DIFFERENCE	$	$	$	$	$	$

Jul	Aug	Sep	Oct	Nov	Dec	Total
						$
						$
						$
$	$	$	$	$	$	$

Jul	Aug	Sep	Oct	Nov	Dec	Total
						$
						$
						$
						$
						$
						$
						$
						$
						$
						$
						$
						$
						$
						$
						$
$	$	$	$	$	$	$

Jul	Aug	Sep	Oct	Nov	Dec	Total
						$
						$
						$
$	$	$	$	$	$	$

CHAPTER 10

Future Planning and Crisis Planning

The secret to financial success is to spend what you have left after saving. Instead of saving what you have left after you spend.

—ANONYMOUS

It is time to set some goals for your future and for times of crisis. We've separated the two because where you put your funds for the future and your funds for a crisis—and how you handle them—may be very different.

Begin as you did with your maintenance plan—evaluate your needs and your wants and set priorities. Most important, learn to appreciate what you have. A plan for future spending must also stay within established bounds. Don't let temptation run amok and thwart your good plan. And above all, don't pay any heed to what neighbors and friends may be doing. Many people spend far too much time and money buying things they don't need to impress people who don't care. If the temptation ever gets too great, take the time to list ten things you are grateful for and, by the time you finish your list, you will have forgotten all the things you don't have.

Above all, keep in mind that you are among the top 10

percent of the world's wealthiest people if you can answer yes to the following questions:

Do I have a choice of what I can eat today?
Do I have more than one pair of shoes?
Do I have a means of transportation?
Do I have a change of underwear?

The Wisdom of Savings

A very vital part of living within your means is to plan adequately for the future and set aside money for a crisis. In this chapter we will discuss some of the strategies involved in these very important plans. Anticipating and saving for future expenses and emergencies is the best insurance you can have for keeping yourself free from the bondage of debt.

Because planning both for future spending and for future crises involve the establishment of savings plans, let's spend a few minutes discussing the wisdom of savings.

Probably the best reason for saving money is control: You will control your future, your security, and your standard of living. Others will not determine control of your money; you will! The road to riches is the same as the road to elimination of debt: It stretches ahead a day at a time, a dollar at a time.

Even though we know that money cannot provide happiness, it can provide security and fewer worries. A nest egg can get you through difficult periods that could strain your marriage, health, and emotional well-being. A savings account is a wise investment.

You should have two forms of savings. First, you need savings that can be easily accessed for needed purchases. Remember the word *needed*. Second, you need savings that are quite *inaccessible*. These are the savings that can remain untouched for years so the value can build and support future and crisis plans. If you're tempted to mix these two savings accounts, be sure to place the funds in different accounts, and perhaps even in different banks. Savings is the lifeblood of wise financial planning and responsibility.

How Do You Save?

In saving money there are three factors that affect your earnings:

The amount saved
The length of time of the investment
The interest rate obtained

Start early to save. Time is one of the greatest assets you have. Have your children open a savings account at an early age.

Making interest work for you is the key. The speed at which savings can grow is illustrated by what economists refer to as the "Rule of 72." They are referring to compound interest. The formula is: 72 divided by the interest rate equals the number of years needed for your savings to double. For example, if you deposited $1,000 in a long-term savings certificate with a yield of 10 percent compound interest, you would divide 72 by 10, which means that your savings will double to $2,000 in approximately 7.2 years.

The following chart will give you an idea of the different interest rates:

		Interest Rate		Time to Double
72	divided by	5%	=	14.4 years
72	divided by	6%	=	12 years
72	divided by	7%	=	10.29 years
72	divided by	8%	=	9 years
72	divided by	9%	=	8 years
72	divided by	10%	=	7.2 years
72	divided by	11%	=	6.55 years
72	divided by	12%	=	6 years

Use Set-Asides

You can use specialized savings accounts, appendages, or suffixes to your bank account to save for specific needs and goals. These are not permanent savings accounts and can even be closed down when the purpose for their existence has passed. Technically, you cannot even refer to these accounts as savings accounts, even though they will accrue interest for the period of time that money is placed into them. You will be putting money into these accounts and drawing it out as needed, depending on the purpose of each individual account. It will give you security to know that for the period of time that you place savings into these accounts you will be earning interest. Your bank or credit union can help you to set up these accounts. You may need to make a visit to their nearest office and ask them what options are available to you.

Let's show you how these accounts can be used. Matt and Julie were young and newly married. Each Christmas season should have been anticipated delight; instead it was anticipated dread. They knew the season was approaching, but each year they seemed to have a longer list of people to buy gifts for with a shrinking pocketbook to pay for it. One day Matt and Julie decided to take control of the Christmas nightmare. They took advantage of a service provided by their bank. They opened a Christmas account. Matt and Julie sat down, took out the checkbook and started to total. Last Christmas they spent $500 for presents. It was $500 they didn't have last December. But Matt and Julie were not going to go into debt for Christmas as they had last year.

To save $500, would require that they set aside $42 every month. If they began in January by putting $42 into a Christmas account, by next December they would have their $500 and they would be debt-free. Matt was paid every two weeks. He knew that his employer offered some options on his direct deposits. He decided to use them. He filled out the proper paperwork, and every two weeks $21 was deposited in his account. He and Julie never even noticed that it was gone. Because there were twenty-six payment periods in a year, he actually saved $542 in a year's time. What's more, the money put into the account had accumulated interest. When Christmas arrived the next year, there were no anxieties and no debts.

Most everyone has learned the value of a Christmas account. That's why we offered it as our first example. Did you ever stop to think that you could do the same thing with every other future financial goal? Did you know that you could save money to realize nearly all your future needs—perhaps even all your future dreams? Let's illustrate.

Dave and Yvonne knew that their car was wearing out. Their present car was bought and paid for. This was good. It allowed them more options. They opened a money market account at their credit union and directly deposited a car payment into it each month. Three years later they had saved enough money, plus interest, to buy a car they were both really excited about and they had cash to pay for it.

Are you beginning to visualize the possibilities? Can you see that it is possible to be debt-free and to remain debt-free? How about recreational vehicles? Have you ever dreamed of one? Or maybe there is some dream vacation, a college education for each of your children, missions for yourself and your children? Dreams know no bounds; and you can afford them when they are planned and saved for.

In addition, you can use set-aside accounts, like your Christmas account, to pay annual peak expenses. We're speaking of those annual budget-busters like taxes, insurance, new appliances, and car maintenance.

Crisis Planning

Just like set-aside accounts can be established for savings, they also work well for crisis planning. A rainy-day account can be set aside for meeting emergency expenses. How big should such an account be? That is up to you, but most experts tell us that as little as 3 percent of your annual take home income will soon build a nice nest egg for an emergency. Whatever you choose to set aside for a rainy day becomes money you won't have to raise when the need arises. You can decide how much you want to contribute and how often you want to contribute and how large you want the account to become. A good rule of thumb suggests having three months of take-home pay set aside for emergencies. This creates a nice little hedge against disaster.

Begin now to be debt-free by establishing specialized savings accounts. Sit down with your family and determine your future goals and designate funds to be put aside for any crisis, a "rainy day fund." Go to your bank or credit union and ask an account representative what options they offer to set aside money in each of your predetermined savings categories. Then, return to your family and set a plan.

Insurance As a Part of Crisis Planning

No discussion of crisis planning would be complete without some mention of the most widely used method of crisis planning—insurance. Insurance is sometimes considered to be one of the least understood and most uninteresting topics of personal finance; yet, who among us can afford to live without it? Whether it be accident, automobile, life, or disability insurance, we all need it. Listen to the counsel of President N. Eldon Tanner:

"Nothing seems so certain as the unexpected in our lives. With rising medical costs, health insurance is the only way most families can meet serious accident, illness, or maternity costs, particularly those for premature births. Life insurance provides income continuation when the provider prematurely dies. Every family should make provision for proper health and life insurance" ("Constancy Amid Change," *Ensign*, November 1979, 82).

Though most of us know we need insurance, many of us are all too often at a loss to understand just how to save money on our insurance needs. Can we have too much insurance, too little, can we waste money by not buying it properly? Here are a few hints if you are in the market for insurance.

Remember that the most beneficial insurance covers the most disastrous of circumstances. Someone once observed that every one of us is within a hair's breath of bankruptcy—all we need to fall over the precipice is a medical catastrophe, a sudden loss of income, or a natural or personal disaster. Therefore, rule number one is *insure for the most catastrophic of circumstances.* Insure yourself from any disaster that might send your family into personal bankruptcy. Insure against disability, against liability for accidents occurring with your car or home, against major medical costs, and against a major lawsuit if you own your own business. In short, insure anything that could completely wipe out everything you own.

Next, *always buy the broadest coverage possible.* Instead of flight insurance, cancer insurance, and accidental death insurance, buy into a good health insurance plan that covers a broad spectrum of major medical needs. Get broad-coverage automobile insurance to cover collision, liability, and personal injury. Obtain a good, solid life insurance policy that will cover you no matter how you happen to die.

Before you buy, shop! shop! shop! Comparing insurance can be like comparing apples and oranges, but a few simple rules cover all policies: Only buy from highly rated companies with proven track records. Take any quote to the Internet and find a consumer organization that allows you to compare prices with other agencies. One such consumer organization is the National Insurance Consumer Organization (NICO). The Internet will probably provide you with more such groups. It would undoubtedly be a mistake to try to list them all, as these organizations come and go. The Internet can provide you with a current list.

Raise your deductible to the highest level you can afford to pay. Raising the deductible will lower the premiums and you can always save the price of the deductible in your rainy-day fund. Just how high should you raise your deductible? That depends on your income and your ability to save. Talk it over with your insurance agent and then decide together how high that level can safely be. Raising the deductible lowers the number of claims you will be tempted to file, so insurance companies like this too. It will keep your insurance rates more affordable.

Last of all, *don't overinsure and don't underinsure.* Make sure you have adequate coverage but don't waste your money on insurance premiums for coverage you don't need. As we cover the different areas of insurance in the Appendix, we'll discuss unnecessary coverage versus necessary coverage.

Saving in a Debt-Free World

It is obvious that the most productive time to save will be when you are completely out of debt. It is only then that dreams will begin to be realized. It is only then that future and crisis plans will take full effect and you will begin to feel completely secure.

Once your debt is under control, you can guarantee your own financial future.

To illustrate the power of savings, suppose, starting at age twenty, you deposited $2,000 a year (or $500 quarterly) for five years into a long-term savings certificate that earns 10 percent interest, compounded quarterly. Then, let's suppose that you leave this money alone without making any further deposits until you reach the age of sixty-five. At the time of your retirement, your original savings investment would be worth $663,878.48. *Just the interest alone would be worth $66,387.85 per year for the rest of your life.* Now that's a nice little salary to add to your pension and/or your social security.

Let's further illustrate this concept. Let's show what the power of savings could mean for you. We'll return to our examination of our fictional family, the Dixons. Remember, they once were $156,645 in debt, not including the interest they would have owed if they had continued to make only the minimum, monthly payments. Over a period of nearly twenty-eight years, they would have expended $321,897 in principal and interest payments. This amount includes a whopping $165,251 of interest alone. At the end of those twenty-eight years, their savings balance would have been $0.00. They would have saved absolutely nothing and would, only then, be at the break-even point. But Dan and Janet stayed on task with their debt-elimination program and were able to pay off all their debts in 9.46 years. With the accelerated retirement of their debt, they realized a savings of $111,054 . That was nice, but it didn't stop there. Dan and Janet went one step further. They began to set aside funds for all their future needs. They took the money they had been using every month as their final power payment—$1,857 a month—and they put it into an interest-bearing account that earned them 6.5 percent interest. In the eighteen and one-half years remaining of the original debt-retirement schedule, they would be able to accumulate a savings of $788,579. Then comes the astounding number. If you add the money saved by retiring their debt early to the amount of money saved over the intervening seventeen years, Dan and Janet Dixon would realize a total turnaround (accumulated savings plus savings on interest) of $899,633. Not bad!

Look at the bottom of the form titled "The Power of Savings—Sample." Dan and Janet estimated how much money they would save in increments of five years. By the time they were ready to retire in twenty years, assuming they did not withdraw any savings over that period, they would have saved $911,202— *that's just under a million dollars!* Is retiring debt early worth it? You be the judge. But keep in mind that 6.5 percent interest may actually be a pretty low figure. With a good, reliable financial planner, Dan and Janet Dixon could do even better than this. Think of the educations, missions, weddings, vacations, and retirement living they will now be able to afford! Dan and Janet's dream can be yours as well.

Are you interested in knowing what the future holds for you? Go to the worksheet titled "The Power of Savings." Access it through the main menu. Take a few minutes and fill in your own figures gleaned from the Debt Elimination Worksheet. Now see how secure your future can be.

THE POWER OF SAVINGS—SAMPLE

STANDARD RETIREMENT OF DEBT

Total payments on largest debt		335 pmts.
Original debt		$ 156,645.49
Total payments over	27.92 years	$ 321,896.87
Total interest paid over	27.92 years	$ 165,251.38
Balance at end of	27.92 years	$ -

ACCELERATED RETIREMENT OF DEBT PLUS SAVINGS

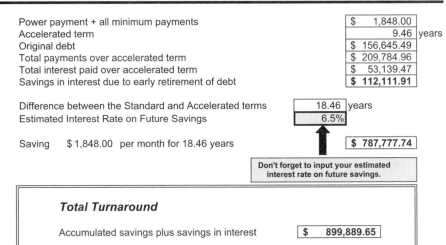

Power payment + all minimum payments	$ 1,848.00
Accelerated term	9.46 years
Original debt	$ 156,645.49
Total payments over accelerated term	$ 209,784.96
Total interest paid over accelerated term	$ 53,139.47
Savings in interest due to early retirement of debt	$ 112,111.91

Difference between the Standard and Accelerated terms	18.46 years
Estimated Interest Rate on Future Savings	6.5%

Saving $ 1,848.00 per month for 18.46 years $ 787,777.74

Don't forget to input your estimated interest rate on future savings.

Total Turnaround

Accumulated savings plus savings in interest $ 899,889.65

NOW YOUR LONG TERM SAVING PLAN:

I will be out of debt in:	9.46	years
I will then deposit:	$ 1,848.00	per month
I will receive:	6.50%	interest

I will have the following savings in:

Five years:	$130,605.49
Ten years:	$311,209.03
Fifteen years:	$560,950.73
Twenty years:	$906,297.88

This could make your future financially secure!

THE POWER OF SAVINGS

STANDARD RETIREMENT OF DEBT

Total payments on largest debt | | pmts.
Original debt | $ |
Total payments over [   ] years | $ |
Total interest paid over [   ] years | $ |
Balance at end of [   ] years | $ |

ACCELERATED RETIREMENT OF DEBT PLUS SAVINGS

Power payment + all minimum payments | $
Accelerated term | | years
Original debt | $
Total payments over accelerated term | $
Total interest paid over accelerated term | $
Savings in interest due to early retirement of debt | $

Difference between the Standard and Accelerated terms [   ] years
Estimated Interest Rate on Future Savings

Saving $ per month for   years $ [   ]

**Don't forget to input your estimated
interest rate on future savings.**

Total Turnaround

Accumulated savings plus savings in interest $ [   ]

NOW YOUR LONG TERM SAVING PLAN:

I will be out of debt in: [   ] years
I will then deposit: $ [   ] per month
I will receive: [   ] interest

I will have the following savings in:

Five years: | $
Ten years: | $
Fifteen years: | $
Twenty years: | $

This could make your future financially secure!

Debt-Free Savings

Once you begin this game of saving money, you'll be surprised how fun and easy it is. As you look over these ideas and try them out, you will find that your ability to save will grow and grow. You're not becoming a tightwad; you're becoming a sensible spender.

It's always best to begin with some overall rules, and here are some good ones to help you get started saving money.

1. Just because you buy everything on sale doesn't mean that you're good at saving money. We knew a woman once who lived for the ads to come out every week. She'd look them over and run for an entire day of shopping pleasure. She had stacks of towels, pillowcases, sheets, and blankets that she'd never use. She had cereals on her shelves piled three deep that usually went stale or were full of bugs before she could use them. She had every gadget known to man, and every member of her family had drawers full of "things" they wondered how they would ever use. What we're saying is that some people think they save money by buying things because they are on sale; but if they can't use them they are not saving money.

Furthermore, sales are not always what they seem to be. Comparison-shopping will show you that the *sale price* at one store may be the *everyday price* at another store. What's more, many items in an ad only appear because the store wishes to feature them, not because they have placed them on sale. Do you know the difference? Sometimes retailers sell their goods when they are about to be discontinued. A discontinued item can be bought at quite a discount; yet, if those items do not carry a full warranty or if parts will no longer be available, your discount will seem mighty puny. A word to the wise: Buy only that which is legitimately on sale, buy only that which is good quality, and above all, buy only that which you can use.

2. When it comes to major purchases, research before you buy. It may take you a little longer, but it never hurts to go from store to store. Take the time to listen to each store's sales pitch on its brand and its good qualities and specifications. Each clerk will provide you with at least one more bit of criteria to consider in your decision process. Listen and write down each and every specification. Consider what the clerk has to say about why his or her store's product is the best. Always ask, "Why should I buy your store's product over another's?" This will help you narrow your search and settle on one particular purchase. Then establish your own set of criteria based on your need and your budget.

Be careful. Just because one product has more bells and whistles than another, it isn't automatically the best product on the market. Take audio speakers for an example. Each clerk will tell you why a particular brand is better than the competitor's. What they won't tell you is that the amps, the decibel levels, and the frequencies of the woofers and the tweeters might be beyond what the human ear is even capable of detecting. Or, perhaps the speakers they are pushing have the capacity to be heard in an entire parking lot, but since you don't live in a parking lot, their capacity exceeds your requirements. Speakers are designed to perform different functions in different settings. Why buy a speaker that has capabilities you will never use?

You might consider a trip to the library to consult buying guides and product evaluations. You need all the help you can get to make wise financial decisions.When the research phase ends, it's time to go to work. Sit down with paper and pencil in hand and prepare to make a decision. If you have a family, be sure to include them if this is a major purchase. Think through all the criteria you have gathered in your research and then decide for yourself. Decide which, out of all the products you've looked at, is the best buy and which will best fit your circumstances at the price you can afford to pay.

3. Check out the retailer. This rule applies to any major purchase. When it comes to groceries or small purchases, such a step is unnecessary, but in major purchases it is wise to know the retailer you are dealing with. Ask other people what experience they have had with a particular retailer or service provider. For more information, call the Better Business Bureau about the store you wish to buy from. This is especially true if it is a small retailer with an unknown reputation. If you have made previous purchases from this retailer, you'll have the benefit of your own personal experience.

What do you look for? Well, do you know anything about the return policy of the store? How about its service record? Can you get fast and efficient repair if the store's merchandise breaks down or does not meet the quality standard they advertised? If you are contracting services, have you asked for references so you can check with someone who has done business with the store before? Be safe, not sorry.

4. Refuse gimmicks. When retailers push their prices down, they have to find a way to make more of a profit some other way.

They could do this by offering service contracts, extended war-ranties, or other little extras that you really don't need. Don't automatically refuse service contracts, extended warranties, or little extras; but remember that sometimes these services aren't worth the extra money. Call someone who provides repairs for this item to see if the price of the contract is worth the extra money. Don't take the contract until you do a little research. Be sure that what is offered you is worth the extra money. It might be that the retailer is making up for the loss on the product price by pushing the service contract.

5. Barter on price. Some retailers may not allow bargaining on price, but you will be surprised how many do. Test the waters by asking first, "Is this a firm price?" If you are given any wiggle room, take it. In addition, it is often good to come with documen-tation or competitor ads that show the same product for a lower price. You might also consider checking the Internet for pricing. Retailers want your business; that is why so many will match or beat the prices of their competitors.

6. Don't buy anything on impulse. The more data you can collect before you make a purchase, the better you'll be. Most of the wasted money in your budget is from impulsive purchases. There are times when you may need to act quickly to take advan-tage of a once-in-a-lifetime price, particularly when quantities are limited, but this is generally not the case. Even in those rare cases you will find that you could have the leeway of a few hours before you need to make your decision.

Take the time to *know before you buy.*

Carefully consider every purchase you make, no matter how small. Sometimes even a split-second thought is all it takes to keep from making a mistake.

Little impulse purchases add up. Buying lunch out every day

instead of brown bagging could cost you as little as $5 a day. But that adds up to $100 a month. Drinking two sodas from a vending machine could cost $30 a month. A magazine or newspaper bought from a newsstand could add up to $100 a year or more. All that money could be put toward your debt and would help you be debt-free. It's a small sacrifice that reaps huge savings.

7. Don't waste your money on a brand name. Sometimes a brand name denotes quality, but ofttimes it means little to nothing when it comes to quality and price. Let us give you an example. Not long ago we happened across a buying guide at our local library. The headline of an article caught our eye. It was an article evaluating polo shirts. What did we learn? Well, the evaluations surprised us. According to research, the best quality, workmanship, and lasting value was the brand of polo shirts sold at a local discount store. Were we surprised? You bet.

This appendix is full of ideas to help you save money—money that can be used against your debt as a power payment and money that can help you build a savings account for future and emergency needs so you remain debt-free. We have included some ideas for saving money in each category of your monthly spending. Look over each section and see how you might be able to save.

Auto and Transportation

- Use public transportation whenever it is feasible.
- Assess your needs before you buy extras for your car.
- Buy and maintain as few vehicles as your family can get by with.
- Hang on to that old car. Today's cars last longer than cars built in the past.
- Buy a safe and comfortable vehicle that accommodates your family's needs without breaking your budget.
- Keep up the maintenance on your vehicle to avoid costly repairs later.
- Drive at a safe and reasonable speed and avoid fast starts and stops.

You can save as much as 50 percent of the energy needed to run your car.

- If your car is stationary for an indefinite period of time, stop the engine.
- Always fill up in the early morning, particularly during the summer months, because gas expands in the heat of the day.
- If you need to run an errand, consider waiting until you can run several errands in one trip and then plot your journey to expend the smallest amount of fuel possible by traveling the fewest miles.
- Keep your car cleaned and your trunk clear. Reducing the weight lowers the consumption of fuel.
- Maintain your car regularly. Under-inflated tires can reduce fuel efficiency by 2 percent for each pound they are under the recommended pressure, plus they wear faster. An engine that has not been tuned up for some time or a clogged air filter can increase fuel needs by 20 percent.
- Running the air conditioner is more fuel efficient than driving with the windows down.
- Fill up with regular unleaded gas unless your owner's manual specifies something else. Regular gas is always cheaper, and higher octane gasoline does your car and your fuel efficiency no extra favors. You're just wasting your money on higher priced gasoline.
- Slow down! Did you know that just by reducing your speed from 70 mph to 65 mph will save you $5 for each hour of driving and about $10 if you are driving a truck or an SUV.
- When you need a mechanic, don't hesitate to shop around and ask for estimates. A reliable, inexpensive mechanic can become your—and your car's—best friend. Find someone who is honest.
- Opt for the monthly rates on parking fares if you need to park on a regular basis. These are much less expensive than daily passes.
- Carpool with four other people. It will cut your driving to once a week and your commuting costs by four-fifths.
- Watch for warranties that are "time prorated." These sort of warranties are offered for tires, batteries, mufflers, shock absorbers, and brakes. Work with companies you can trust. Shop around before you buy and learn from your past mistakes.
- Before buying a recreational vehicle, consider the strength of your commitment to use it. Too many people own RVs that sit idle for

fifty weeks a year. If you don't intend to use a recreational vehicle frequently, rent one.

Charity and Contributions.

- Remember that the payment of tithes and offerings is part of successful financial management: "Successful financial management in every LDS home begins with the payment of an honest tithe. If our tithing and fast offerings are the first obligations met following the receipt of each paycheck, our commitment to this important gospel principle will be strengthened and the likelihood of financial mismanagement will be reduced. Paying tithing promptly to Him who does not come to check up each month will teach us and our children to be more honest with those physically closer at hand" "Marvin J. Ashton, "Guide to Family Finance," *Liahona,* April 2000, 42).

- Consider giving generously to the United Way. One of the advantages of giving to a conglomerate charity such as the United Way is that it reduces the amount you expend in individual, door-to-door contributions. Your local United Way consolidates payments to a variety of charities and it has a proven track record.

- Always give to known and well-respected charities. Be leery of charities you have never heard of. Listen carefully to telephone solicitations or for solicitors who give names similar to well-known and well-respected charities. Unscrupulous vendors often adopt names that sound similar to known entities. So if it sounds similar but isn't the same—don't give.

- Ask the solicitor what percentage of your donation will actually go to its intended recipients. Unscrupulous charities have high overhead and pay overly large and unusual wages to their leadership. If the overhead exceeds the money received by the recipient, stay away.

- Allot yourself a set amount of money you can afford to donate every month. There are many worthy charities, and you are not required to give to them all. Decide which charities to give to before they come asking.

- Be wary of any charity that sells low-quality goods at inflated prices. Such items are probably not things you need or will use. Both you and your charity may better benefit by a direct donation than from a purchase sold at an inflated price.

- Donate your excess goods to secondhand thrift stores that benefit the needy and provide them with employment opportunities. Such stores include Deseret Industries—operated by The Church of Jesus Christ of Latter-day Saints—Goodwill Industries, or the Salvation Army.

- Ask for receipts for any time, money, or goods that you have donated. Determine the value of your donation by comparing it to similar goods sold at the local thrift store. Such donations can be deducted from your income taxes, but be sure to check the tax law before you take any deduction.

- When you need a service, hire people in need that you know personally or come highly recommended, then both of you will benefit.

Debit and Credit Cards

- Avoid those cards that carry a balance with interest. Use only those cards that are paid in full at the end of every month, or debit cards that are deducted directly from your bank account much like a plastic check, but without the cost of a printed check.

- If you should need a card with a credit balance, make it a practice to pay your balance in plenty of time to avoid late fees or additional interest.

- There are some cards that offer "cash back" advantages if they are paid before a certain date. Such cards can be advantageous to you if you are good at discipline and self-control. Pay these bills as soon after you receive them as you can to maximize your savings.

- If you can't keep your monthly credit balance at zero and control your spending on credit cards, then cut them up, nuke them in your microwave, or freeze them in a block of ice so they have to be unthawed before using so that you can control your spending.

- If you do a lot of business travel, ask your business to provide you with a credit card for your business travel needs. Never expend personal funds for business needs.

- Prevent identity theft and erroneous charges. Carefully and thoroughly review your credit card statements every month and verify each purchase. Look for hidden costs you didn't anticipate. Dispute any erroneous charges. Be aware of every charge and report anything that looks like identity theft or credit card fraud.

- Pay your credit card bills on time. If you find yourself in a situation where you absolutely need to get a loan, consult your life insurance policies, your retirement plan, or an IRA and try to borrow from your own resources. Better to owe yourself than to owe others.

- If you do need to take out a loan, pay it back as quickly as you can. Even small debts are too much debt when it drains the interest from your budget. Once you are out of debt, never return.
- Save for big purchases. There is joy in anticipation. Cash always affords you dealing power, and that equates with greater savings.

Education

- Use your local library. The public library is an excellent place to read any number of valuable books. Not only do libraries offer books, but they offer audiocassettes, CDs, books on tape, videos, artwork, and duplication equipment. Owning a library card is one of the best cost-saving investments you can make. Before you spend, consult your library.
- Look for book exchanges if you want to own books. Libraries, bookstores, the Internet, and shopping malls can offer places to trade used books for ones you want to acquire.
- Be selective if there is a fee associated with belonging to a club, organization, or extra-curricular activity that interests you. Evaluate both the time and cost commitment to determine if your money is well spent. Some activities enhance education while others detract. Spend when the investment value is the greatest and never spend more than you can afford.
- Newspapers can be cost effective and timely information sources. But never buy at the newsstand; take a subscription. It costs much less than buying at the rack, and coupons are not usually offered with newsstand copies of a newspaper.
- If you subscribe to a magazine, do not resubmit your payment the first time they ask for a renewal. By taking your time, you often are offered substantial discounts to keep your subscription. You can oversubscribe to magazines and newspapers, so only buy what you can afford and what will offer you the maximum savings. Ask about two-year and three-year subscription rates; such rates are often deeply discounted.
- If your child wants to play a musical instrument, start with a rental to see if he or she enjoys it or will stay committed to it before you purchase. If possible, rent an instrument with an option to buy, or check garage sales for used instruments rather than investing in a new one.
- Shop before you commit to lessons for your children. Ask your

friends for the names of competent instructors. Inquire about rates before you make a commitment.

- Pianos can be found in classified ads, and often for a lower price than when purchased from a dealer. But if you buy this way, make sure that you are paying a fair price and that the instrument is in good shape. It pays to take an experienced musician with you to make the best choice.

- Make saving for your children's college education a top priority in your family. Put money aside into long-term savings. This qualifies as a worthy "future" plan. Private school tuition and college costs can be saved. Check with a tax preparation expert for tax-sheltered savings plans.

- Good grades translate into cost savings in the form of scholarships. Help and encourage your student to work hard and perform to the best of his or her ability.

- Paper, pencils, and supplies are offered for lower prices at discount stores. Watch for sales, especially seasonal sales, and buy enough to last the school year where possible.

- Take advantage of free tests offered by state institutions to find areas of interest or aptitude.

- Watch for government publications, extension service classes, and other publications that can add to your education. The government encourages education and offers any variety of wonderful publications to aid you in your educational pursuits.

- Keep an eye open for business-sponsored workshops, seminars, conventions, special schooling, and so forth. You can often transfer these added credentials into added income to your budget.

- Become educated in your areas of interest or hobbies. Hobbies and pastimes can be converted into secondary income.

- Community education classes are offered in local school districts and libraries. Brochures are often mailed to your home offering these free or low-cost classes.

- Without the growing edge of advanced education, you can end up as the low man on the totem pole when promotions at work come along. Management teams like new ideas, abilities, and initiative. Take advantage of educational opportunities. These may be as attractive as offers of cash.

Food

- Carefully plan your meals.
- Keep your eye out for the weekly grocery specials and savings.
- Get a little exercise at the supermarket. Look more than just at the shelves at eye level. Those shelves above and below eye level often contain the best deals.
- Sales on food items are cyclical. Eventually, every grocery item you are accustomed to purchasing will go on sale. Buying food at its lowest, cyclical price and buying enough to last until the price goes down again saves you a great deal of money in your monthly food budget. This can be done without abandoning your favorite stores or your favorite brands.
- Be aware that not everything mentioned in the weekly ad is a sale item.
- Perishable foods that can be purchased only on a weekly basis should be consumed when they are "in season" and plentiful.
- Can or freeze perishables for greater longevity. Purchase canned goods, meat, and frozen items in large enough quantities to last for quite a while.
- Know how much to purchase without going past the expiration date. A good way to discover how much food will be adequate for your food storage is to mark your package with a date of purchase. Then when the item is fully consumed, you can easily assess how many of that particular item you will use in a year's time.
- Use your computer as another asset in your search for lower food prices. Use the Sunday newspaper to acquaint yourself with the coupons offered for the week; then match the coupons with the sale items listed on the website of your favorite store. Most of the major grocery chains maintain a website, and many independent supermarkets form co-ops.
- Look for "loss leaders," weekly specials your grocery store offers to entice shoppers inside. The retailer hopes you will come into his store to buy these special items, some of which may even be offered at prices lower than his own costs, then purchase many more items at regular prices. If you buy enough, the retailer can make up for his loss on those few featured items. When your budget is tight and you live close to several different markets, you could use this to your advantage by shopping more than one store for "loss leaders." This will save you significantly as long as the stores are close. If the price

of gasoline exceeds the amount you save at the grocery store, try sticking closer to home.

- Keep your pantry fully stocked. A fully stocked pantry of food purchased at its lowest price allows you the flexibility to still serve your family delicious meals while continuing to purchase only weekly sales items. This strategy could cut your grocery bill nearly in half and increase your food storage.

- When you must purchase something that is not on sale, look and compare price and quality on different brands. You can often find little-known brands with comparable quality and taste to the more well-known brand names. Store brands are, for the most part, less expensive than national brands.

- Take advantage of unit pricing. Most stores list a unit price next to the sticker price. Unit pricing helps you compare prices for different brands packaged in different sized containers.

- Remember that items placed in displays at the end of aisles are not necessarily items on sale.

- Don't buy on impulse. Plan what you will buy before you enter the store. Work from a list.

- If you tend to be distracted in the grocery store, leave the distractions at home. Small children lose patience and make you start buying things you didn't intend to.

- Remember that shopping on an empty stomach can be as big a distraction to you as chubby little hands. You'll put many more items in your cart when you are hungry than when you have a full stomach.

- Use coupons. But be aware that some retailers will raise the price of the coupon item to make up the shortfall. Have a good head for prices.

- Limit your trips to the store to once a week. Even better, try to limit your trips to every other week or even once a month where that is possible.

- Non-food items are sometimes less expensive when purchased at stores other than the supermarket.

- Don't be loyal to anything but price.

Gifts

- Use your yearly financial plan to anticipate when and whom you might be required to buy a gift for each month.

- Set aside money each month for all your gift expenses.
- Use special savings to purchase gift items as you discover them on sale. Or buy them in bulk to keep on hand when gift-giving opportunities arise.
- Adopt the philosophy that a wedding anniversary does not have to be an expensive celebration. Wedding anniversaries can be observed by traditions that your family budget can accommodate. Establish traditions that are thoughtful and romantic without needless expense. A husband could surprise his wife with breakfast in bed. A wife could serve a candlelight dinner for two. One or two roses or a whole bouquet of flowers from the local supermarket may be just as welcome as an expensive present. A thoughtful and heartfelt card expressing your feelings for your spouse might be more appreciated and treasured than a costly anniversary present.
- Look for closeouts on wrapping paper and bows. After Christmas is always a good occasion. Look for plain, non-seasonal type paper that you can use inexpensively. Save your wrapping paper and bows in a big drawer, if you have the room, and get more than one use out of it. In addition, make a trip periodically to a printing establishment in your town and purchase roll-ends to use as gift wrap.
- Become familiar with "sales seasons." Keep those "seasons" in mind as you budget. A year's experience with your budget can teach you when to find items at their lowest price. Plan to spend money in the month you anticipate a sale. You can even make your purchases a year in advance if the price just happens to be right.
- Knickknacks, figurines, perfumes, socks, and earrings are small items that close out periodically and are so small they may not even be advertised. You might run into such a sale on a routine outing. Watch for closeouts. Being in the right place, at the right time, with money in the bank can help you save money.
- Don't overlook homemade gifts. Those gifts made by you come from your heart and can be treasured long after the store-bought gifts break or fade away.
- Buy small gifts at the dollar store.
- Establish a set-aside or a Christmas account to save for Christmas purchases.
- Consider an office fund where everyone is asked to pool a few dollars every month for get-well gifts or flowers for births, weddings, and deaths. Such office funds can cost very little and save the whole office a great deal.

- Try neighborhood or group gift-buying pools to save money for wedding gifts.
- Be creative. One woman makes and gives thank-you notes as gifts at wedding showers and birth announcements to give at baby showers. Scrapbook pages, attractively wrapped baskets of small, inexpensive useful items, baskets of food supplies, and useful, homemade gifts can be made into attractive, inexpensive, and greatly appreciated gifts for friends and family.

Home and Shelter

- Be happy with what you have. We waste an incredible amount of time and money trying to impress people who don't really care. "Use it up, wear it out, make it do, or do without."
- When an appliance breaks down, don't be foolish enough to think that this entitles you to a brand new appliance. Always check to see if the appliance can be repaired first before you go out and make a new purchase. Ask the repairman to estimate how much it would cost to fix your appliance. If the cost of the repair is neither close to nor exceeds the cost of a new appliance, then, by all means, fix your old appliance first.
- Look for good used appliances, perhaps from a neighbor or friend who is moving. In addition, check the classified ads or look for good garage or estate sales. One family we are acquainted with bought a refrigerator for a third of what a new refrigerator would have cost, and has now had that same refrigerator for the last fifteen years. They made a wise choice. But always carefully inspect used appliances and make certain they are in good working order. If you can't afford new, buy used.
- As with all purchases, whether it be new or used, buy it to last. Check durability records from consumer advocacy groups either at the library or on the Internet.
- When you've made a purchase, be sure to save the receipts and the warranties. We cannot tell you how many times the warranty on an appliance and the receipt of purchase saved us from having to buy a new appliance. The repairs were covered by the warranty and the cost to us was minimal.
- Cleaners don't have to be expensive. Check your library for books on cleaning solutions that can be made at home. Sometimes vinegar and ammonia, which can be purchased inexpensively, will clean as well as an expensive formula cleaner.

- Use the library as a good resource for books on house-cleaning shortcuts. Shortcuts can save both time and money as well as the maintenance and repair of your household possessions.

Insurance

- If your employer offers accident insurance as part of your benefits package, you'd be foolish to opt out. But if you have to buy it yourself, don't. If you die, your death is just as valuable to your survivors whether you die from cancer and heart attack or whether you die in an accident. There is no additional benefit from accidental death insurance.

- Disability insurance is vital. The ability to bring home a paycheck is more valuable to your family than any other single thing. The most important type of insurance is not auto, health, or homeowners; it is a disability policy. Many employers not only offer disability insurance, they also pay the premiums for you. If you don't have a disability policy now, go out and purchase one.

- Most states require that you carry an insurance policy on your automobile. Any number of companies provide automobile insurance, and many offer discounts if you have a homeowner's policy with them. When looking for automobile insurance, price should not be the only consideration. Check the company's claim record.

- Avoid vehicles that require higher than average insurance premiums. Check the insurance premium before you buy a new car.

- Ask the agent about discounts for auto insurance. Are there "good student" rates? "Non-drinker" rates? "Good driver" rates? Ask what discounts are available and which you qualify for.

- Remember that your car insurance is no better than your agent. A warm, friendly, compassionate insurance agent is worth his or her weight in gold. Find someone who will be an advocate for you and fight in your behalf.

- The age of your vehicle should determine the amount of insurance coverage you have. If there is little difference between the value of the car and the deductible on the insurance, it would not be wise to take maximum coverage. But, before dropping any area of coverage, make sure that liability, personal injury, and theft are adequately covered. Your agent can best advise you what level of coverage your specific car should require.

- Make sure you carry a homeowner's policy that adequately covers your home and your possessions. Does the policy offer full replacement value?

- If you are renting, buy a rental insurance policy. It will offer you the same sort of coverage offered to homeowners and will protect you from major catastrophes.

- To avoid a hassle should you need to file a claim, it is a good idea to videotape each room of your home, showing all your personal belongings. Your memory is not as good as you think. In addition, record serial numbers on expensive belongings such as computers, televisions, major appliances, and so on. Then put these inventories somewhere off the premises, preferably in a safety deposit box, where they can be retrieved in an emergency.

- If an accident or damage occurs to your home or rental unit, check the policy to see if the cost of your damages is covered. Many homeowners pay premiums for years, and then when shingles blow off the roof in a storm or the children spill red punch on the brand new carpet, they fail to realize that their homeowner's policy covers the damages.

- Most families cannot get by without adequate health insurance coverage. If you are self-employed and cannot afford insurance, then just purchase major medical insurance and be sure that it includes some sort of maternity benefits if you are in your childbearing years. Check the deductibles and keep a savings where possible to meet the deductible expenses which sometimes can be fairly large.

- Work through an insurance broker if you don't have access to group rates. A broker works for several different companies and can, therefore, find you the best rates available.

- Don't be afraid of HMOs or PPOs. HMO plans require that you see only their physicians, PPO plans allow you to see other physicians but at a reduced rate of coverage.

- Don't buy any health plan that carries a lifetime maximum benefit. Some plans with a lifetime maximum of $1,000,000 seem adequate enough on the surface, but with today's rising medical costs, that amount is quickly consumed when there is a real emergency.

- Life insurance is an absolute necessity. How much do you need? You can estimate that by multiplying your gross income by 80 percent if you are a low-income earner, by 70 percent if you are a middle-income earner, and by 60 percent if you are a high-income earner. To that figure add the cost of college educations and the mortgage on your home.

- Always buy term insurance rather than cash value life insurance. Term insurance is less costly on the whole and much more beneficial. Whole-life policies are often encouraged for their money-saving value, but you could save far more than their value by investing the premiums you would have placed in the cash value policy into a moderate, secure investment—even a CD has a better yield than a whole-life policy.
- If the down payment on your home is less than 20 percent, your mortgage company will require mortgage insurance. You must pay the premium until your equity in the home reaches 20 percent. Be sure to cancel your mortgage insurance when your equity reaches this point. Federal regulations require your lender to notify you when your equity reaches 22 percent. But you can save months of premiums by taking the initiative and contacting your leader before it reaches this point. You can also use your life insurance policy to protect your mortgage.
- Don't buy travel insurance. If you buy your plane tickets using credit cards that offer automatic travel insurance, or by purchasing traveler's checks that automatically offer insurance, you are covered. Some travel agencies also provide automatic travel insurance when you book through them.
- Never be a sucker for the hard-sell sales pitch. Don't be frightened into buying policies because the insurance salesman is trying to clinch a sale and you do not understand what you are buying.

Leisure and Recreation

- If you have cable or satellite television, sit down with your family and determine which package of channels best suits your family's tastes and budget. Limiting the number of channels reduces your monthly bill. Watch for specials and discounts on installation and take advantage of "special package" offerings.
- If your family watches too much television, doesn't watch it much at all, or if your budget cannot afford pay television, then unhook this costly expense. You can always rent an occasional videotape or DVD for entertainment instead.
- If you and your family enjoy regular trips to the gym, shop for a facility that is near to your home and has the lowest fees and the best options to suit your family's needs and tastes. But beware of sign-up fees and fine print that mandates the length of your commitment. Some gyms appear to have lower monthly rates but when factoring

in their sign-up fees, you actually expend far more money. Many gyms in corporate areas offer discounts that make working out near work instead of home a much better deal. And remember, sometimes buying your own home fitness equipment may be a good investment over the lifetime of your fitness commitment.

- Take advantage of public facilities and community recreation centers.
- Participate in sports that don't require expensive gear.
- Rent or borrow sports equipment that you use only occasionally.
- Buy sports equipment at yard sales, or watch for good buys in the classified section of your newspaper.
- Join a local sports group for enthusiasts of bicycling, rafting, running, and so on. These groups sponsor competitions and keep you informed of upcoming activities (many of which are at little or no cost), and they often rent or sell equipment at discounted rates.
- Develop interests in things that are low-cost and provide family fun. These could include visiting public parks, hiking, writing, painting, woodcarving, scrapbooking, and so on. Keep the amount reasonable, flexible, and well within your price range.
- Check your community schools for inexpensive classes that teach skills or provide a recreation experience.
- Attend discount matinees or buy discount tickets at your bank, credit union, or grocery customer service center.
- Watch for $1 or $2 movie theaters where movies play at the end of their theatrical runs. You may have to wait longer to see them, but the price might better suit your family's budget.
- Don't be afraid to use the pay-per-view feature of your cable or satellite network. This will allow you video prices before release dates.
- Wait for the video release on some movies. Watching movies from the safety of your home can also help you screen the violence and sexual content of some PG and PG-13 rated movies.
- Never waste money on a movie that embarrasses you or is not enjoyable. Read newspaper reviews, talk to trusted friends, and check out sites on the Internet that give thorough reviews of film content.
- Use the library. Public libraries also rent videotapes and DVDs. The cost is nothing and the rental time is extended for a week at a time.
- Get a copy of your community activity calendar. Take advantage of free or discounted concerts, art museums, lectures, and other special activities.

- If eating out gets too expensive, pack a picnic and eat in the park.
- Search for deals. Scan the newspaper for coupons and discount nights at local restaurants.
- Ask for a children's menu or dine out on family discount nights. Restaurants have enticements to bring in diners.
- Check the appetizer menu. A soup or salad with an appetizer could be a great meal and it could cut your dining-out budget by 10 percent or more.
- If the restaurant is known for its huge portions, consider buying one meal and sharing it.
- Buy quality toys that children will use and wear out. Check for durability and safety. Avoid toys with detachable pieces that can be lost or swallowed.
- Give up any kind of recreation where the costs are more excessive than your income allows. But don't give up things your family can do and enjoy together. Those days and hours of fun will be the moments your children will cherish for a lifetime.

Medical

- Remember that preventative dental care will save you more than any other thing when it comes to caring for your teeth.
- Check your bills and ask about any charges that seem excessive.
- Be prudent about when and how often you visit your doctor. Don't be guilty of either not going often enough or going too often.
- Develop a regular exercise program to make you more disease-resistant and healthy. Don't give up exercise for the sake of money. Find ways to incorporate it within your lifestyle. For example, if you are accustomed to buying lunch at the office every day, try packing your own lunch and working out during your lunch hour. Even a walk through a mall every day at lunch time will keep you fit.
- If it is not a medical emergency, before having tests or surgery, get a second opinion, and contact your insurance company. Use your insurance company's contract physicians whenever possible.
- Find a doctor you can trust, and if you don't like the particular doctor you've chosen, don't be afraid to ask around and find another one.
- Don't use the emergency room unless it's an emergency. Wait until regular office hours or use an after-hours medical center. Many health care providers are associated with such emergency centers.

- Always review a hospital bill. Dispute any excessive charges or services you did not receive. Don't count on your insurance company doing this for you. When you catch an error they are always grateful.
- When purchasing prescription drugs, use a pharmacy that regularly substitutes lower-cost generics for brand-name prescription drugs. Use mail order pharmacies where you can buy a three-month supply of any long-term prescription need. Don't be shy about asking your doctor for samples, particularly if you are in a financial crunch or the prescription is costly. Pharmaceutical companies frequently leave samples of their products with physicians.
- If your pharmaceutical company sends you literature about any diagnosed illness that requires prescription medication, read them thoroughly and follow their advice to keep your future medical costs lower.
- Take advantage of any health programs or evaluations offered by your employer or given through special community clinics or health evaluations. Flu shots, mammograms, and cholesterol and diabetes testing are often provided at reduced rates.

Other/Miscellaneous

- Trade baby-sitting duties with another parent who has children of similar ages.
- If you are going out for the evening and need in-home baby-sitting, be effective with your time. Shorten the time you are gone to lessen the expense of childcare.
- Be extremely careful when selecting a daycare provider. Cheaper is rarely better. If, however, you are going through a university's childcare service, you'll likely get both cheaper rates and higher quality. Don't be hesitant to check out the local university for preschool/daycare needs, even if you and your spouse are not affiliated with the university. Most offer reduced rates because some of their providers are students in training and because government programs provide subsidies to university preschools and daycares that help parents attend school while their children are cared for. Almost all programs are open first to students, but then open to the general population at a low rate. Shop for quality, distance from home, and friendliness of the environment for your children.
- Analyze your financial situation. Sometimes the cost of daycare eats up such a large percentage of your second paycheck that it hardly pays to work.

- Teach your children money management skills by setting an allowance for your children. Let it be within your ability to pay.
- Having a pet to take care of can be a good opportunity for a child to learn money management. Pets and pet care give children good opportunities for growth and for caring for someone or something other than themselves.
- When looking for a pet, check local animal shelters and classified ads, as well as pet stores. Remember, however, that some pets are very high maintenance in spite of their initial price. Only maintain a pet you can reasonably afford.
- Remember that letters and e-mails are less expensive than long-distance phone calls.
- When sending packages, investigate several alternatives for shipment. Rates vary.
- Do not buy books on how to save money. Instead, borrow them from the library.
- Avoid buying from door-to-door salesmen or from phone solicitors. Such salespeople cannot be easily checked for references.
- Use the "Board of Directors approach" to handling high-pressure sales pitches, especially for big purchases. That is just our term for checking things out with your family first. Any purchase over an established amount, like say $50 to $100, must be approved with your spouse and perhaps even the family as a whole. Also, time is on your side; don't ever rush into a purchase.
- Consider purchasing some items cooperatively with family, friends, or neighbors. So long as such cooperative purchases do not threaten your relationships, they can save you a lot of money. Group buys of camping equipment, boats or recreational vehicles, snow-blowers, and so on could save you some money.
- Send for government publications on how to save money. You can obtain a catalog on-line or from Consumer Information Center-D, P.O. Box 100, Pueblo, Colorado 81002.

Personals

- If you have the skill and talent, you could learn how to cut your children's hair. If you lack the skill and know-how, take your family to a competent cosmetology school where students provide hair care for minimal prices.
- Consider buying your shampoo in bulk from a beauty supply house

that allows sales to the public. Or make it a practice to only buy shampoo and other hair care needs when they go on sale.

- Cleanliness and neatness are more important than expensive clothing, makeup, or hairstyles. Proper care costs little money. Don't skimp on hygiene.
- Remember that all products—be they toothpaste, deodorant, soap, mouthwash, or first-aid supplies—go on sale. Remember that the best buys are often found at discount and warehouse stores.

Savings and Investments

- Find a good financial counselor. Keep shopping until you find the right one for you. Then, follow his or her advice to manage your savings and investments.
- If your employer offers savings, investment plans, or retirement savings where they pick up a portion of the cost or match funds, always take advantage of it.
- Remember that markets are volatile. Be safe and sure in your investment choices.
- Money Market Certificates are higher-yielding savings accounts than passbook savings. Compare options.
- Consult with the Social Security Administration for a report on your benefit status in order to prepare for your retirement. Each year the Social Security Administration is required to send you a report of your Social Security earnings.
- Do not count on Social Security to provide all your retirement needs. Social Security needs supplemental savings to provide adequate retirement coverage. How much more will you need? Consult your investment counselor or search the Internet for retirement calculators that can assist you in determining an amount.

Taxes

- Always be honest when it comes to paying taxes. Taxes are the price we pay for citizenship. Pay your taxes honestly and cheerily. Keep good records so that your tax deductions are fair and accurate.
- Keep records and receipts. Itemizing deductions will usually save more money than taking standard deductions.
- Take time to accurately fill out the W-4 form that you file with your employer. Periodically check this form to see if it is still accurate. Neither have too much money withheld nor too little. Try to get as

small a refund as you can. You are better served to save money in passbook savings than use your tax refund like a savings account.

- If possible, consider doing your own taxes or purchasing tax software to help you calculate the amount of your taxes. Self-employed individuals or others who have complicated returns need the help of a tax professional and you should not hesitate to use a professional. The money is well spent. Accountant's fees are deductible from your taxes.

- Send for publications from the IRS to help you find ways to save money on next year's taxes. Tax laws change almost yearly. Keep current.

- Keep all your records for at least five years in case of an audit. This will save you money and avoid penalties.

- Don't go into debt to save money on taxes or to pay taxes. Remember that you'll always save money by putting your taxes into a savings account rather than an escrow account.

- Report any earnings such as interest or money paid to you for which you did not receive a W-2. Keep good records so that you can honestly report any additional income and to verify income if you are audited.

- If you have questions, ask a tax professional or call the IRS.

- Don't use your tax refunds unwisely. Plan for their usage just as you do any other additional income.

Utilities

- Unplug idle appliances when not in use and when feasible. TVs, VCRs, CD players, microwave ovens, and so on will continue to use small amounts of electricity when not in use and cost consumers about $3 billion annually.

- Keep your laundry room door shut when the dryer is in use—particularly in air-conditioning season. A dryer uses air to dry the clothes inside. You will force your dryer to work harder—not to mention your air-conditioning system—when the door to the laundry is left open.

- Since 85 percent of the energy used to wash clothes goes to heating the water, use cold water and cold-water detergents to wash clothes. Switching from hot water to cold will cut your energy consumption in half.

- Switch to compact fluorescent lighting. Bulbs cost more, but they expend only one-fourth of the energy and last ten times longer. Just replacing four 100-watt bulbs with four 23-watt compact fluorescent bulbs will save $80 over three years.

- Ask your gas and electric companies for a comparison analysis of your yearly expenses and usage. This may enable you to find where you can find waste and inefficiency.
- Check with your local utility company for pamphlets on money-saving ideas.
- Turn your water heater down to 110° F. to save on heating water.
- Clean furnace filters about every two months. Consider cleaning your heating ducts.
- Invest in a programmable thermostat and adjust your heating and cooling temperatures automatically. Turn temperatures higher or lower, depending on the season, the time you are home versus not at home, and the times you are asleep.
- Keep your home properly insulated and properly caulked for air leaks that add to heating and cooling costs.
- Before buying furnace or air-conditioning units, check the Seasonal Energy Efficiency Ratio (SEER) for air conditioning and the equivalent for furnaces. An increase of each rating point results in 10 percent more efficiency.
- Get the right furnace and air conditioner for your home. One that is too powerful will reduce efficiency as will one that is not powerful enough.
- Shop for long-distance telephone service.
- Avoid impulsive long-distance calls; these add up fast.
- Consider using a cell phone for long distance calls if you can save money by doing so.
- Review the options charged to your telephone bill. Eliminate any unnecessary extras and consult your phone company for package discounts.
- Take short showers instead of baths. You'll use less water.
- Don't overwater your lawns and gardens.
- Install drip irrigation systems for gardens. You'll cut water usage and weed growth.
- Never water in the heat of the day. Watering your lawn between 10 A.M. and 6 P.M. just invites more water evaporation than water seeping into the soil.

Vacations and Travel

- Prepare a grub box to take on a trip. You can make sandwiches and snacks, store them safely in a cooler, and avoid unnecessary stops at stores or at expensive restaurants and cafés.
- Check for discount booklets, coupons, or group pricing for hotel services. When checking prices, be sure you ask about taxes or hidden fees.
- Look through online travel services for good deals.
- Camp out. Camping is much less expensive than motels and hotels.
- Book online and save.
- Take several short vacations—short in terms of time and distance. Check out nearby national and state parks where visits are inexpensive and sights are breathtaking.
- Rent rather than own recreational vehicles unless you plan on using them extensively.
- Book with a tour instead of individually. Look for low-cost fares far in advance; be patient and be flexible.
- If not in a hurry, travel standby or agree to give up your seat if the flight is overbooked. If you are bumped you are usually given hotel and even the price of another ticket for your future use.
- Take advantage of frequent flyer miles. Keep your records and receipts.
- Visit an area during its off-season for discount rates and smaller crowds.
- Shop around for prices of tickets and other amusements in the area you plan to visit.
- Get help from travel clubs for maps and lodging rates. It may cost you a fee to join, but could save money in the long run.
- Write or visit the area Chamber of Commerce online for tourist information.

Wardrobe

- Watch for special sales. But avoid temptation by only checking the clothing ads when you are in the market for something.
- Buy at the end of the season for next year's clothing.
- Look for seconds, blemishes, or irregulars. These items are often generously discounted. Retailers are prohibited by law from selling you a second with an irregularity that will affect its wear.

- Don't be afraid to ask for a discount on the price.
- Never go to a clothing sale without a spending limit.
- Take advantage of hand-me-downs. Trade with neighbors and friends.
- Shop at thrift or consignment stores for quality used clothing.
- Invest in a sewing machine. Making your own clothing can be fun as well as useful.
- Check catalog sales. You can often purchase brand name clothing much cheaper through the catalog.

Now that you have completed this book, it is time to apply the principles, get rid of that debt, and become financially secure. We have provided you with a certificate of achievement on the CD-ROM to print out as soon as your goal of being debt-free has been met. Print it out, have it framed, and place your Declaration of Financial Independence in a prominent place in your home. It will not only provide satisfaction to you but establish you as a role-model for your children to carry on this tradition from generation to generation.

Index

Abernathy, Durant, 12
Amortization tables, 14
Appliances, saving money on, 169
Ashton, Marvin J.: on managing money, 5; on interest, 14–15; on living within your means, 80
Assets, selling/trading/cashing in, 45–46

Balance transfers, 46–49
Bankruptcy: Chapter 7 protection, 56; as a last resort, 56; Chapter 13 protection, 56–57; debts not erased by, 57; perils of, 57; recovering from, 57–58
Bartering on price, 159
Benson, Ezra Taft: on incurring debt, 11; on good debt, 12
Brand names, being cautious about, 160
Budgeting. *See* Maintenance plans; Monthly plans; Planning; Yearly plans

Calculating your real indebtedness (Step 2): formula for, 23, 25; example, 23–25; Debt Elimination Worksheet, Step 2— How Far Are You Really in Debt? (sample worksheet), 24. *See also* Identifying your debts (Step 1); Making power payments (Step 3)
Cash, carrying, 82–83
Cashing in assets, 45–46
Chapter 7 Bankruptcy, 56
Chapter 13 Bankruptcy, 56–57
Charitable contributions, saving money on, 162–63
Christmas accounts, 147–49
Clark, J. Reuben, on interest, 15
Clothing, saving money on, 180–81
Compound interest, 146
Credit cards: impact on Americans' consumer debt, 4–5; scrimping/saving and, 9; transferring balances on, 46–49; impact of high interest rates, 48–49; saving money on, 163–64
Credit counseling services: choosing a service, 53–55; advantages and disadvantages of using, 55–56
Crisis planning: definition of, 72; using savings accounts for, 149; N. Eldon Tanner on, 149–50; insurance as part of, 149–51. *See also* Future planning

Daycare/baby-sitting, saving money on, 175
Debit cards, saving money on, 163–64

Debt: Joseph F. Smith on getting out of, 1, 9–10; America as a nation of, 3–4; urbanization and de-personalization of American society and, 4; advent of credit cards and, 4–5; as an addiction, 5; Gordon B. Hinckley on getting out of, 7; conquering discouragement over, 7–8; definition of, 8–9; Benjamin Franklin on, 9; credit as, 9; impact of modern advertising on, 9; Ezra Taft Benson on incurring, 11; as a major problem in American society, 11–12; Ezra Taft Benson on good, 12; good vs. bad, 12–13; including both principal and interest when calculating, 14; freedom from, 16; Gordon B. Hinckley on self-reliance and, 17; prevalence of, regardless of income level, 17; Thomas S. Monson on having a year's supply and being free of, 27; Steve Rhode on, 53
Debt consolidation loans, 49–51
Debt elimination, alternative methods of: selling, trading, or cashing in assets, 45–46; transferring balances, 46–49; debt consolidation loans, 49–51; home equity loans, 51–52; advantages of making power payments vs. alternative methods, 52–53; credit counseling services, 53–56; bankruptcy, 56–58
Debt elimination process: getting help from extended family members, 19; involving your spouse and children in, 19; summary of, 19–20; managing the process yourself vs. using a credit counselor, 44–45. See also Calculating your real indebtedness (Step 2); Identifying your debts (Step 1); Making power payments (Step 3)

Debt Elimination Worksheet, Step 3—How Long for Payoff? (blank worksheet), 41
Debt Elimination Worksheet, Step 3—How Long for Payoff? (sample worksheet), 30, 39
Debt Elimination Worksheet, Step 1—Identification of Debts (blank worksheet), 40
Debt Elimination Worksheet, Step 1—Identification of Debts (sample worksheet), 22, 38
Debt Management Rules, 15–16
Debts, identifying. See Identifying your debts (Step 1)
Debt-to-income ratio, 18
Declaration of Financial Independence, 181
Dixon Family Yearly Financial Plan (sample worksheet), 102–3

Education, saving money on, 164–65
"Evaporation," avoiding money, 82–83

Food, saving money on, 166–67
Franklin, Benjamin, 9
Future planning: definition of, 72; evaluating needs/wants and setting priorities, 144; appreciating what you have, 144–45; savings accounts as a vital part of, 145; easily accessed vs. inaccessible savings accounts, 145–46; making interest work for you, 146, 151–53; using set-aside accounts, 147–49; The Power of Savings (sample worksheet), 154; The Power of Savings (blank worksheet), 155. See also Crisis planning

Gifts, saving money on, 167–69
Gimmicks, refusing, 158–59
Grant, Heber J., on living within your means, 10, 59
Groceries, saving money on, 166–67

Hinckley, Gordon B.: on managing money, 6; on getting out of debt, 7; on self-reliance and debt, 17; on money as the root of troubles in marriage, 61; on financial planning, 71, 72

Home equity loans, 51–52

Home expenses, saving money on, 169–70

Honesty, 67–68

How Much Are You Worth? (blank worksheet), 88

Hunter, Howard W.: on being frugal and avoiding self-indulgences, 10; on indebtedness, 10

Identification of Yearly Peak Expenses (blank worksheet), 86

Identification of Yearly Peak Income (blank worksheet), 87

Identifying your debts (Step 1): listing your debts, 20; ranking loans by interest rate and paying off the highest interest rate loan first, 20–21; determining the number of payments remaining, 21; example, 21–23; Debt Elimination Worksheet, Step 1—Identification of Debts (sample worksheet), 22, 38; Debt Elimination Worksheet, Step 1—Identification of Debts (blank worksheet), 40. See also Calculating your real indebtedness (Step 2); Making power payments (Step 3)

Impulse spending, avoiding, 81–82, 159–60

Indebtedness, Howard W. Hunter on tragedy of, 10

Indebtedness, calculating your real. See Calculating your real indebtedness (Step 2)

Insurance: as an element of crisis planning, 149; N. Eldon Tanner on, 149–50; buying the broadest possible coverage, 150; insuring for the most catastrophic of circumstances, 150; getting the right coverage, 151; setting a high deductible, 151; shopping before you buy, 151; saving money on, 170–72

Interest: as a companion to debt, 9; as a fee for renting money, 13; vs. principal, 13; as a component of your monthly payment, 13–14; Marvin J. Ashton on, 14–15; collecting vs. paying, 15; J. Reuben Clark on, 15; Rule of 72, 146; compound, 146

Interest Gap, 25–26

Investments/savings, saving money on, 177

Kimball, Spencer W., on worshipping material things, 1–2

Last Month's Income and Spending (blank worksheet), 89–92

Maintenance plans: key to, 80; reason for having, 80; keeping expenses lower than income, 81; avoiding impulse spending, 81–82, 159–60; paying as you go, 82; keeping money "evaporation" to a minimum, 82–83; determining last month's spending and income, 83; identifying peak expense periods, 84; identifying peak income periods, 84; determining your total worth, 85; Identification of Yearly Peak Income (blank worksheet), 87; Identification of Yearly Peak Expenses (blank worksheet), 86; How Much Are You Worth? (blank worksheet), 88; Last Month's Income and Spending (blank worksheet), 89–92. See also Monthly plans; Yearly plans

Major purchases, researching,
157–58
Making power payments (Step 3):
Debt Elimination Worksheet,
Step 1—Identification of Debts
(sample worksheet), 22, 38; using
10–15% of your income, 27–28;
making out your power payment
check, 28; applying the power
payment check to your shortest
debt, 28–29; paying off the
shortest debt, 29; example,
29–36; Debt Elimination
Worksheet, Step 3—How Long
for Payoff? (sample worksheet),
30, 39; increasing your power
payment and paying off the next
debt, 31; Power Payment Plan
(sample worksheet), 34–35;
implementing your power
payment plan, 36–37; Debt
Elimination Worksheet, Step 1—
Identification of Debts (blank
worksheet), 40; Debt Elimination
Worksheet, Step 3—How Long
for Payoff? (blank worksheet), 41;
Power Payment Plan (blank
worksheet), 42–43. See also
Calculating your real
indebtedness (Step 2); Identifying
your debts (Step 1)
Material things: Spencer W. Kimball
on worshipping, 1–2; as a source
of personal identity, 4; Howard
W. Hunter on coveting, 10
Medical expenses, saving money on,
174–75
Money: as an indispensable part of
life, 1; Henrik Ibsen on, 2;
Gordon B. Hinckley on money as
the root of troubles in marriage,
61
Money, saving. See Saving money
Money management: inability of
Americans to meet basic financial
needs, 2–3; Marvin J. Ashton on,
5; Gordon B. Hinckley on, 6;

Heber J. Grant on living within
your means, 10, 59;
acknowledging your need for
improvement, 61; Pre-
Assessment Quiz on basic money
management issues, 62–66;
Marvin J. Ashton on living within
your means, 80
Monson, Thomas S., on having a
year's supply and being debt-free,
27
Monthly payments, 13–14
Monthly plans: importance of,
93–94; being patient, 94;
individuality of, 94; including
flexibility in, 94–95; yearly plans
as the basis for, 105; example,
105–6, 111, 116–19, 124–32;
using The Plan worksheet,
106–9; using The Tally
worksheet, 109–10; using the
Yearly Record of Finances
worksheet, 110; The Plan
(sample worksheet), 116–19; The
Plan (blank worksheet), 120–23;
The Tally (sample worksheet),
124–32; The Tally (blank
worksheet), 133–41; Yearly
Record of Finances (blank
worksheet), 142–43. See also
Yearly plans
Morrison, Alexander B., on the
purpose of becoming self-reliant,
60

Needs. See Wants and needs

Paying as you go, 82
Peak expense periods, 84
Peak income periods, 84
Personal care, saving money on,
176–77
Planning: recording and analyzing
weekly income and expenses, 68;
setting up a record-keeping
system, 68; making a detailed
family plan, 69; Gordon B.

Hinckley on, 71, 72; types of plans, 71–72. *See also* Crisis planning; Future planning; Maintenance plans; Monthly plans; Yearly plans
Power Payment Plan (blank worksheet), 42–43
Power Payment Plan (sample worksheet), 34–35
Power payments, making. *See* Making power payments (Step 3)
Pre-Assessment Quiz (basic money management issues), 62–66
Price, bartering on, 159
Principal, 13

Quizzes and surveys: Pre-Assessment Quiz (basic money management issues), 62–66; Survey of Needs and Wants, 74–79

Real indebtedness, calculating your real. *See* Calculating your real indebtedness (Step 2)
Record-keeping systems, importance of, 68
Recreation, saving money on, 172–74
Researching major purchases, 157–58
Retailers, checking out, 158
Rhode, Steve, 53
Rule of 72, 146

Sales and sale prices, 156–57
Saving money: avoiding impulse spending, 81–82, 159–60; avoiding buying just because something is on sale, 156; comparing sale and everyday prices, 156–57; researching major purchases, 157–58; checking out retailers, 158; refusing gimmicks, 158–59; bartering on price, 159; being cautious about brand names, 160; on vehicles and transportation, 160–62; on charitable contributions, 162–63; on debit and credit cards, 163–64; on education, 164–65; on food, 166–67; on gifts, 167–69; on appliances, 169; on home expenses, 169–70; on insurance, 170–72; on recreation, 172–74; on medical expenses, 174–75; on daycare/baby-sitting, 175; on personal care, 176–77; on savings/investments, 177; on taxes, 177–78; on utilities, 178–79; on vacations/travel, 180; on clothing, 180–81
Savings accounts: as a vital part of future planning, 145; easily accessed *vs.* inaccessible, 145–46; factors affecting earnings, 146; power of, 146, 151–53; Rule of 72, 146; using set-aside accounts, 147–49; for crisis planning, 149; The Power of Savings (sample worksheet), 154; The Power of Savings (blank worksheet), 155
Savings/investments, saving money on, 177
Self-reliance: Gordon B. Hinckley on debt and, 17; as a basic doctrine and practice, 59–60; Alexander B. Morrison on the purpose of, 60; Brigham Young on the importance of, 60; planning and, 61
Selling assets, 45–46
Set-aside savings accounts, 147–49
Smith, Joseph F., on getting out of debt, 1, 9–10
Survey of Needs and Wants, 74–79
Surveys. *See* Quizzes and surveys

Tanner, N. Eldon, on preparing for the unexpected, 149–50
Taxes, saving money on, 177–78
Term, loan, 13–14
The Plan (blank worksheet), 120–23
The Plan (sample worksheet), 116–19

The Power of Savings (blank
worksheet), 155
The Power of Savings (sample
worksheet), 154
The Tally (blank worksheet), 133–41
The Tally (sample worksheet),
124–32
Things to Remember (blank
worksheet), 114–15
Things to Remember (sample
worksheet), 100–101
Total worth, 85
Trading assets, 45–46
Transferring balances, 46–49
Transportation, saving money on,
160–62
Travel/vacations, saving money on,
180

Utilities, saving money on, 178–79

Vacations/travel, saving money on,
180
Vehicles, saving money on, 160–62

Wants and needs: risks of failing to
distinguish between, 69–70;
definition of needs, 70;
importance of discussing with
your spouse, 70, 72–73; difficulty
of drawing a clear line between,
70–71; Survey of Needs and
Wants, 74–79
Worksheets, blank:
Debt Elimination Worksheet,
Step 1—Identification of Debts,
40;
Debt Elimination Worksheet,
Step 3—How Long for Payoff?,
41;
Power Payment Plan, 42–43;
Identification of Yearly Peak
Income, 87;
Identification of Yearly Peak
Expenses, 86;
How Much Are You Worth?,
88;

Last Month's Income and
Spending, 89–92;
Yearly Financial Plan, 112–13;
Things to Remember, 114–15;
The Plan, 120–23;
The Tally, 133–41;
Yearly Record of Finances,
142–43;
The Power of Savings, 155
Worksheets, sample:
Debt Elimination Worksheet,
Step 1—Identification of Debts,
22, 38;
Debt Elimination Worksheet,
Step 3—How Long for Payoff?,
30, 39;
Power Payment Plan, 34–35;
Things to Remember,
100–101;
Dixon Family Yearly Financial
Plan, 102–3;
The Plan, 116–19;
The Tally, 124–32;
The Power of Savings, 154

Yearly Financial Plan (blank
worksheet), 112–13
Yearly plans: importance of, 93–94;
being patient, 94; individuality of,
94; including flexibility in, 94–95;
basing next year's spending on
last year's expenses, 95;
anticipating the needs of the
coming year, 95–96; example,
96–104; Things to Remember
(sample worksheet), 100–101;
Dixon Family Yearly Financial
Plan (sample worksheet), 102–3;
Yearly Financial Plan (blank
worksheet), 112–13; Things to
Remember (blank worksheet),
114–15. *See also* Monthly plans
Yearly Record of Finances (blank
worksheet), 142–43
Young, Brigham, on the importance
of self-reliance, 60

About the Authors

Lyle and Tracy Shamo have made a hobby of debt management and stretching household dollars. Lyle has been a frequent lecturer on this subject to bank and credit union clientele, church groups, and community gatherings throughout Utah and Idaho. Tracy spent a year discussing household finances on a Salt Lake City radio station. Both adhere to the belief that you can be debt-free, regardless of income.

Lyle is managing director of the Audiovisual Department of The Church of Jesus Christ of Latter-day Saints. He has a master's degree in instructional science and media and a bachelor's degree in speech and public address. Both degrees are from Brigham Young University. In addition to serving in four stake presidencies and twice as a bishop, Lyle has been a high councilor, Young Men president, elders quorum president, and many times a teacher.

Tracy is a homemaker, mother of eight, and grandmother of six. She has a bachelor's degree in speech and dramatic arts from Brigham Young University. She has served in many church callings but most enjoys those that involve teaching. She has written numerous scripts for Church movies and videos and currently serves with Spence Kinard as co-host of "Concerts from Temple Square," a radio program of music produced by The Church of Jesus Christ of Latter-day Saints.